COMPLETE BOOK OF

Grade 2

P9-CWE-984

THINKING KIDS®

An Imprint of Carson-Dellosa LLC
P.O. Box 35665 • Greensboro, NC 27425 USA
carsondellosa.com

Thinking Kids®
Carson-Dellosa Publishing LLC
P.O. Box 35665
Greensboro, NC 27425 USA

Printed in the USA • All rights reserved.　　　　　　　　　ISBN 978-1-4838-1307-3

07-100171120

Dear Parents, Caregivers, and Educators,

The *Complete Book* series provides young learners an exciting and dynamic way to learn the basic skills essential to learning success. This vivid workbook will guide your student step-by-step through a variety of engaging and developmentally appropriate activities in phonics, reading comprehension, math, problem solving, and writing.

The *Complete Book of Grade 2* is designed for learning reinforcement and can be used as a tool for independent study. This workbook includes:

- High-interest lessons.
- Easy-to-understand examples and directions.
- Challenging concepts presented in simple language.
- Review lessons to measure progress and reinforce skills.
- Expanded teaching suggestions to guide further learning.

To find other learning materials that will interest your young learner and encourage school success, visit www.carsondellosa.com

4

Table of Contents

READING **5**

All About Me! 6
Consonants 7–12
Consonant Blends and Teams 13–23
Short and Long Vowels 24–36
Compound Words 37–39
Contractions 40–42
Syllables 43–45
Suffixes and Prefixes 46–50
Reading for Details 51–53
Sequencing and Tracking 54–59
Classifying 60–66
Comprehension Skills 67–82
Fiction and Nonfiction 83–86

ENGLISH **87**

ABC Order 88–90
Synonyms, Antonyms, and Homophones 91–97
Nouns, Pronouns, and Subjects 98–107
Verbs, Predicates, and Parts of a Sentence 108–114
Adjectives and Articles 115–117
Sentences 118–121
Ownership 122–123
Dictionary Skills 124–126

SPELLING **127**

Number Words 128–129
Short- and Long-Vowel Words 130–139
Verbs, Animals, and Family Words 140–145
Location Words, Opposites, and Time Words 146–152

MATH **153**

Patterns 154–155
Ordinal Numbers 156
Addition and Subtraction 157–175
Graphs 176–177
Multiplication 178–179
Fractions 180–181
Geometry 182–184
Measurement, Time, and Money 185–201
Problem Solving 202–204

GLOSSARY **205–210**

TEACHING SUGGESTIONS **211–223**

ANSWER KEY **224–256**

Reading

All About Me!

Directions: Fill in the blanks to tell all about you!

Name _____

             (First)   (Last)

Address _____

City _____ State _____

Phone number _____

Age _____

Places I have visited: _____

_____

_____

_____

_____

My favorite hobbies: _____

_____

_____

_____

Let's Begin: b, c, d, f, g, h, j

Directions: Fill in the beginning consonant for each word.

Example: __c__ at

__b__ ox

__j__ acket

__g__ oat

__h__ ouse

__d__ og

__f__ ire

Let's Begin: k, l, m, n, p, q, r

Directions: Write the letter that makes the beginning sound for each picture.

_____

_____

_____

_____

_____

_____

_____

_____

_____

_____

_____

_____

Let's Begin: s, t, v, w, x, y, z

Directions: Write the letter under each picture that makes the beginning sound.

_____

_____

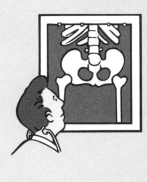

_____

_____

_____

_____

_____

Last Letters: b, d, f, g

Directions: Fill in the ending consonant for each word.

ma __d__

cu __b__

roo __f__

do __g__

be __d__

bi __b__

Last Letters: k, l, m, n, p, r

Directions: Fill in the ending consonant for each word.

nai **l**

ca **n**

gu **m**

ca **r**

truc **k**

ca **p**

pai **l**

Last Letters: s, t, x

Directions: Fill in the ending consonant for each word.

ca __t__

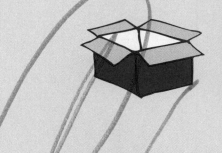

bo __x__

bu __s__

fo __x__

boa __t__

ma __t__

Bring on the Blends!

Consonant blends are two or three consonant letters in a word whose sounds combine, or blend. **Examples: br, fr, gr, pr, tr**

Directions: Look at each picture. Say its name. Write the blend you hear at the beginning of each word.

_____

_____

_____

_____

_____

_____

_____

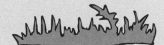

_____

_____

_____

_____

_____

Blends: fl, br, pl, sk, sn

Blends are two consonants put together to form a single sound.

Directions: Look at the pictures and say their names. Write the letters for the beginning sound in each word.

_____

_____

_____

_____

_____

_____

_____

_____

_____

_____

Blends: bl, sl, cr, cl

Directions: Look at the pictures and say their names. Write the letters for the beginning sound in each word.

__cl__own   __bl__anket   __cr__ayon

__cl__ock   __sl__ide   __cl__oud

__sl__ed   __cr__ab   __cr__ocodile

Tell Me a Riddle

Directions: Write a word from the word box to answer each riddle.

clock	blow	climb	slipper
gloves	clap	blocks	flashlight

1. You need me when the lights go out.
   What am I? _____

2. People use me to tell the time.
   What am I? _____

3. You put me on your hands in the winter to keep them warm.
   What am I? _____

4. Cinderella lost one like me at midnight.
   What am I? _____

5. This is what you do with your hands when you are pleased.
   What is it? _____

6. You can do this with a whistle or with bubble gum.
   What is it? _____

7. These are what you might use to build a castle when you are playing.
   What are they? _____

8. You do this to get to the top of a hill.
   What is it? _____

Teammates

Consonant teams are two or three consonant letters that have a single sound. **Examples: sh** and **tch**

Directions: Write each word from the word box next to its picture. Underline the consonant team in each word. Circle the consonant team in each word in the box.

bench	match	shoe	thimble	shell
peach	watch	whale	chair	wheel

  _____

_____

_____

  _____

_____

_____

_____

_____

_____

Join the Team

Directions: Look at the first picture in each row. Circle the pictures that have the same sound.

whistle

shoe

chin

thumb

Sort It Out

Directions: Look at the words in the word box. Write all of the words that end with the **ng** sound in the column under the picture of the **ring**. Write all of the words that end with the **nk** sound under the picture of the **sink**. Finish the sentences with words from the word box.

strong   rank   bring   bank   honk   hang   thank

long   hunk   song   stung   bunk   sang   junk

_____   _____

_____   _____

_____   _____

_____   _____

_____   _____

_____   _____

_____   _____

1. _____ your horn when you get to my house.

2. He was _____ by a bumblebee.

3. We are going to put our money in a _____.

4. I want to _____ you for the birthday present.

5. My brother and I sleep in _____ beds.

Shhh! Silent Letters

Some words have letters you can't hear at all, such as the **gh** in **night**, the **w** in **wrong**, the **l** in **walk**, the **k** in **knee**, the **b** in **climb** and the **t** in **listen**.

Directions: Look at the words in the word box. Write the word under its picture. Underline the silent letters.

knife	light	calf	wrench	lamb	eight
wrist	whistle	comb	thumb	knob	knee

_____   _____   _____

_____   _____   _____

_____   _____   _____

_____   _____   _____

Review

Directions: Read the story. Circle the consonant teams (two or three letters) and silent letters in the underlined words. Be sure to check for more than one team in a word! One has been done for you.

One day last (Spring) my family went on a picnic. My father picked out a pretty spot next to a stream. While my brother and I climbed a tree, my mother spread out a sheet and placed the food on it. But before we could eat, a skunk walked out of the woods! Mother screamed and scared the skunk. It sprayed us with a terrible smell! Now, we think it is a funny story. But that day, we ran!

Directions: Write the words with three-letter blends on the lines.

_____

_____

_____

_____

Double Duty: Hard and Soft c

When **c** is followed by **e**, **i** or **y**, it usually has a **soft** sound. The **soft c** sounds like **s**. For example, **c**ircle and fen**c**e. When **c** is followed by **a** or **u**, it usually has a **hard** sound. The **hard c** sounds like **k**. For example, **c**up and **c**art.

Directions: Read the words in the word box. Write the words in the correct lists. One word will be in both. Write a word from the box to finish each sentence.

pencil	cookie	dance	popcorn	cent
circus	lucky	mice	tractor	card

Words with soft c	**Words with hard c**
pencil	_____
_____	_____
_____	_____
_____	_____
_____	_____
	_____

1. Another word for a penny is a _____.

2. A cat likes to chase _____.

3. You will see animals and clowns at

   the _____.

4. Will you please sharpen my _____?

Double Duty: Hard and Soft g

When **g** is followed by **e**, **i** or **y**, it usually has a **soft** sound. The **soft g** sounds like **j**. **Example:** change and gentle. The **hard g** sounds like the **g** in **g**irl or **g**ate.

Directions: Read the words in the word box. Write the words in the correct lists. Write a word from the box to finish each sentence.

engine	glove	cage
magic	frog	giant
flag	large	glass
goose		

Words with soft g   **Words with hard g**

_____engine_____   _____

_____   _____

_____   _____

_____   _____

_____   _____

1. Our bird lives in a _____.

2. Pulling a rabbit from a hat is a good

   _____ trick.

3. A car needs an _____ to run.

4. A _____ is a huge person.

5. An elephant is a very _____ animal.

Letter Detector: Short Vowels

Vowels can make **short** or **long** sounds. The **short a** sounds like the **a** in c**a**t. The **short e** is like the **e** in l**e**g. The **short i** sounds like the **i** in p**i**g. The **short o** sounds like the **o** in b**o**x. The **short u** sounds like the **u** in c**u**p.

Directions: Look at each picture. Write the missing short vowel letter.

p _u_ p   n _e_ t   s _o_ ck

_a_ x   l _i_ ps   h _a_ t

f _o_ x   t _e_ nt   p _i_ n

Super Silent e

Long vowel sounds have the same sound as their names. When a **Super Silent e** appears at the end of a word, you can't hear it, but it makes the other vowel have a long sound. For example: **tub** has a **short** vowel sound, and **tube** has a **long** vowel sound.

Directions: Look at the following pictures. Decide if the word has a short or long vowel sound. Circle the correct word. Watch for the **Super Silent e!**

can (cane)   (tub) tube   rob (robe)

(pin) pine   (cap) cape   not (note)

slid (slide)   dim (dime)   tap (tape)

Letter Detector: Long Vowels

Directions: Say the name of the pictures. Listen for the long vowel sounds. Write the missing long vowel sound under each picture.

c ____ ke   h ____ ke   n ____ se

____ pe   c ____ be   gr ____ pe

r ____ ke   b ____ ne   k ____ te

Review

Directions: Read the words in each box. Cross out the word that does not belong.

long vowels

cube

cup

rake

me

short vowels

man

pet

fix

ice

long vowels

soap

seed

read

mat

short vowels

cat

pin

rain

frog

Directions: Write **short** or **long** to label the words in each box.

_____ vowels

hose

take

bead

cube

eat

see

_____ vowels

hose

take

bead

cube

eat

see

R in Charge

When a vowel is followed by the letter **r**, it has a different sound.

Example: he and **her**

Directions: Write a word from the word box to finish each sentence. Notice the sound of the vowel followed by an **r**.

park	chair	horse	bark	bird
hurt	girl	hair	store	ears

1. A dog likes to _____.

2. You buy food at a _____.

3. Children like to play at the _____.

4. An animal you can ride is a _____.

5. You hear with your _____.

6. A robin is a kind of _____.

7. If you fall down, you might get _____.

8. The opposite of a boy is a _____.

9. You comb and brush your _____.

10. You sit down on a _____.

Double Trouble

Usually when two vowels appear together, the first one says its name and the second one is silent.

Example: bean

Directions: Unscramble the double vowel words below. Write the correct word on the line.

 ocat _____

 mtea _____

 teas _____

 ogat _____

 atli _____

 etar _____

 eetf _____

 otab _____

 spea _____

 apil _____

Team Time: ou, ow, au, aw

The vowel teams **ou** and **ow** can have the same sound. You can hear it in the words **clown** and **cloud**. The vowel teams **au** and **aw** have the same sound. You hear it in the words **because** and **law**.

Directions: Look at the pictures. Write the correct vowel team to complete the words. The first one is done for you. You may need to use a dictionary to help you with the correct spelling.

__au__ to   cl ____ n   h ____ se

fl ____ er   s ____   ____ l

p ____ der   m ____ th   j ____

Team Time: ea

The vowel team **ea** can have a **short e** sound like in **head**, or a **long e** sound like in **bead**. An **ea** followed by an **r** makes a sound like the one in **ear** or like the one in **heard**.

Directions: Read the story. Listen for the sound **ea** makes in the bold words.

Have you ever **read** a book or **heard** a story about a **bear**? You might have **learned** that bears sleep through the winter. Some bears may sleep the whole **season**. Sometimes they look almost **dead**! But they are very much alive. As the cold winter passes and the spring **weather** comes **near**, they wake up. After such a nice rest, they must be **ready** to **eat** a **really** big **meal**!

words with long ea

_____

_____

_____

_____

words with short ea

_____

_____

_____

ea followed by r

_____

_____

_____

Team Time: ie, ei, eigh, ey

The vowel team **ie** makes the **long e** sound like in **believe**. The team **ei** also makes the **long e** sound like in **either**. But **ei** can also make a **long a** sound like in **eight**.

Directions: Circle the **ei** words with the **long a** sound.

neighbor	veil	receive
reindeer	reign	ceiling

The teams **eigh** and **ey** also make the **long a** sound.

Directions: Finish the sentences with words from the word box.

obey   weigh   thief   field   ceiling

1. Rules are for us to _____.

2. The bird got out of its cage and flew up to the _____.

3. How much do you _____?

4. They caught the _____ who took my bike.

5. Corn grows in a _____.

Team Time: oi, oy, ou, ow

Directions: Look at the first picture in each row. Circle the pictures that have the same sound.

oil

toy

couch

howl

Team Time: ai, ee

Directions: Write in the vowel team **ai** or **ee** to complete each word.

r ____ ____ n

f ____ ____ d

s ____ ____ d

p ____ ____ l

s ____ ____ l

cr ____ ____ k

Review

Directions: Read the story. Fill in the blanks with words from the word box.

cookies   Joe   bowl   tooth   flour   eight

spoon   eats   enjoys   round   boy   either

Do you like to cook? I know a _____

named _____ who loves to cook. When

Joe has a sweet _____, he makes

_____. He puts _____

and sugar in a _____ and stirs it with a

_____. Then, he adds the butter and

eggs. He makes cookies that are _____

or other shapes. He likes them _____

way. Now is the part he _____ the

most: Joe _____ the cookies. He might

eat seven or _____ at a time!

That's Y!

When **y** comes at the end of a word, it is a vowel. When **y** is the only vowel at the end of a one-syllable word, it has the sound of a **long i** (like in **my**). When **y** is the only vowel at the end of a word with more than one syllable, it has the sound of a **long e** (like in **baby**).

Directions: Look at the words in the word box. If the word has the sound of a **long i**, write it under the word **my**. If the word has the sound of a **long e**, write it under the word **baby**. Write the word from the word box that answers each riddle.

happy	penny	fry	try	dry
bunny	windy	sky	party	fly

my   **baby**

_____   _____

_____   _____

_____   _____

_____   _____

_____   _____

1. It takes five of these to make a nickel. _____

2. This is what you call a baby rabbit. _____

3. It is often blue and you can see it if you look up. _____

4. You might have one of these on your birthday. _____

Putting It Together

Compound words are two words that are put together to make one new word.

Directions: Read the sentences. Fill in the blank with a compound word from the box.

raincoat   bedroom   lunchbox   hallway   sandbox

 1. A box with sand is a

_____.

 2. The way through a hall is a

_____.

 3. A box for lunch is a

_____.

 4. A coat for the rain is a

_____.

 5. A room with a bed is a

_____.

What's Cooking?

Compound words are formed by putting together two smaller words.

Directions: Help the cook brew her stew. Mix words from the first column with words from the second column to make new words. Write your new words on the lines at the bottom.

grand	brows
snow	light
eye	stairs
down	string
rose	book
shoe	mother
note	ball
moon	bud

1. _____

2. _____

3. _____

4. _____

5. _____

6. _____

7. _____

8. _____

Two-for-One Special

Directions: Draw a line under the compound word in each sentence. On the line, write the two words that make up the compound word.

1. A firetruck came to help put out the fire.

_____

2. I will be nine years old on my next birthday.

_____

3. We built a treehouse at the back.

_____

4. Dad put a scarecrow in his garden.

_____

5. It is fun to make footprints in the snow.

_____

6. I like to read the comics in the newspaper.

_____

7. Cowboys ride horses and use lassos.

_____

Short and Sweet

Contractions are a short way to write two words, such as **isn't**, **I've** and **weren't**. **Example: it is = it's**

Directions: Draw a line from each word pair to its contraction.

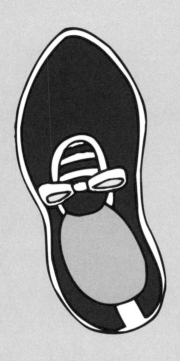 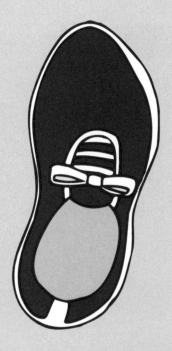

I am	she's
it is	they're
you are	we're
we are	he's
they are	I'm
she is	it's
he is	you're

We Love Contractions!

Directions: Cut out the two words and put them together to show what two words make the contraction. Glue them over the contraction.

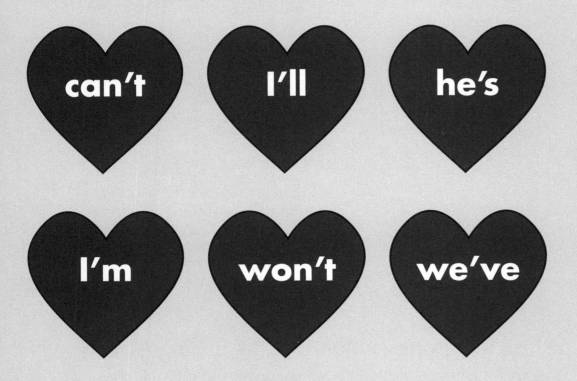

- -

cut out

This page is blank for the cutting activity
on the opposite side.

Put Your Hands Together

Words are made up of parts called **syllables**. Each syllable has a vowel sound. One way to count syllables is to clap as you say the word.

Example:

cat	1 clap	1 syllable
table	2 claps	2 syllables
butterfly	3 claps	3 syllables

Directions: "Clap out" the words below. Write how many syllables each word has.

movie _____

piano _____

tree _____

bicycle _____

sun _____

cabinet _____

football _____

dog _____

basket _____

swimmer _____

rainbow _____

paper _____

picture _____

Give Me a Break

Dividing a word into syllables can help you read a new word. You also might divide syllables when you are writing if you run out of space on a line. Many words contain two consonants that are next to each other. A word can usually be divided between two consonants.

Directions: Divide each word into two syllables. The first one is done for you.

kitten   <u>   **kit   ten**   </u>

lumber   _____

batter   _____

winter   _____

funny   _____

harder   _____

dirty   _____

sister   _____

Break it Up!

When a double consonant is used in the middle of a word, the word can usually be divided between the consonants.

Directions: Look at the words in the word box. Divide each word into two syllables. Leave space between each syllable. One is done for you.

butter	puppy	kitten	yellow
dinner	chatter	ladder	happy
pillow	letter	mitten	summer

<u>but</u> <u>ter</u>   _____   _____

_____   _____   _____

_____   _____   _____

_____   _____   _____

Many words are divided between two consonants that are not alike.

Directions: Look at the words in the word box. Divide each word into two syllables. One is done for you.

window	doctor	number
mister	winter	pencil
barber	sister	picture

<u>win</u> <u>dow</u>   _____   _____

_____   _____   _____

_____   _____   _____

Add It On

A **suffix** is a syllable that is added at the end of a word to change its meaning.

Directions: Add the suffixes to the root words to make new words. Use your new words to complete the sentences.

help + ful = _____

care + less = _____

talk + ed = _____

love + ly = _____

loud + er = _____

1. My mother _____ to my teacher about my homework.

2. The radio was _____ than the television.

3. Sally is always _____ to her mother.

4. The flowers are _____.

5. It is _____ to cross the street without looking both ways.

Backward Nan

Directions: Read the story. Underline the words that end with **est**, **ed** or **ing**. On the lines below, write the root words for each word you underlined.

The funniest book I ever read was about a girl named Nan. Nan did everything backward. She even spelled her name backward. Nan slept in the day and played at night. She dried her hair before washing it. She turned on the light after she finished her book—which she read from the back to the front! When it rained, Nan waited until she was inside before opening her umbrella. She even walked backward. The silliest part: The only thing Nan did forward was back up!

1. _____

2. _____

3. _____

4. _____

5. _____

6. _____

7. _____

8. _____

9. _____

10. _____

11. _____

12. _____

13. _____

The Three Rs

Prefixes are syllables added to the beginning of words that change their meaning. The prefix **re** means "again."

Directions: Read the story. Then, follow the instructions.

Kim wants to find ways she can save the Earth. She studies the "three R's"—reduce, reuse and recycle. Reduce means to make less. Both reuse and recycle mean to use again.

Add **re** to the beginning of each word below. Use the new words to complete the sentences.

_____ build   _____ fill

_____ read   _____ tell

_____ write   _____ run

1. The race was a tie, so Dawn and Kathy had to

   _____ it.

2. The block wall fell down, so Simon had to

   _____ it.

3. The water bottle was empty, so Luna had to

   _____ it.

4. Javier wrote a good story, but he wanted to

   _____ it to make it better.

5. The teacher told a story, and students had to

   _____ it.

6. Toni didn't understand the directions, so she had to

   _____ them.

Prefix Power

Directions: Change the meaning of the sentences by adding the prefixes to the **bold** words.

The boy was **lucky** because he guessed the answer **correctly**.

The boy was (un) _____ because he

guessed the answer (in) _____.

When Mary **behaved**, she felt **happy**.

When Mary (mis) _____,

she felt (un) _____.

Mike wore his jacket **buttoned** because the dance was **formal**.

Mike wore his jacket (un) _____

because the dance was (in) _____.

Tim **understood** because he was **familiar** with the book.

Tim (mis) _____ because he was

(un) _____ with the book.

Review

Directions: Read each sentence. Look at the words in **bold**. Circle the prefix and write the root word on the line.

1. The **preview** of the movie was funny.

   _____

2. We always drink **nonfat** milk.

   _____

3. We will have to **reschedule** the trip.

   _____

4. Are you tired of **reruns** on television?

   _____

5. I have **outgrown** my new shoes already.

   _____

6. You must have **misplaced** the papers.

   _____

7. Police **enforce** the laws of the city.

   _____

8. I **disliked** that book.

   _____

9. The boy **distrusted** the big dog.

   _____

10. Try to **enjoy** yourself at the party.

    _____

Mike's Bike

Directions: Read the story about bike safety. Answer the questions below the story.

Mike has a red bike. He likes his bike. Mike wears a helmet. Mike wears knee pads and elbow pads. They keep him safe. Mike stops at signs. Mike looks both ways. Mike is safe on his bike.

1. What color is Mike's bike? _____

2. Which sentence in the story tells why Mike wears pads and a helmet? Write it here.

   _____

   _____

3. What else does Mike do to keep safe?

   He _____ at signs and

   _____ both ways.

Total Recall

Directions: Read about Nikki's pets. Then, answer the questions.

Nikki has two cats, Tiger and Sniffer, and two dogs, Spot and Wiggles. Tiger is an orange striped cat who likes to sleep under a big tree and pretend she is a real tiger. Sniffer is a gray cat who likes to sniff the flowers in Nikki's garden. Spot is a Dalmatian with many black spots. Wiggles is a big furry brown dog who wiggles all over when he is happy.

1. Which dog is brown and furry? _____

2. What color is Tiger? _____

3. What kind of dog is Spot? _____

4. Which cat likes to sniff flowers? _____

5. Where does Tiger like to sleep? _____

   _____

6. Who wiggles all over when he is happy?

   _____

Nikki's Garden

People on the Go

Directions: Read the story about different kinds of transportation. Answer the questions with words from the story.

People use many kinds of transportation. Boats float on the water. Some people fish in a boat. Airplanes fly in the sky. Flying in a plane is a fast way to get somewhere. Trains run on a track. The first car is the engine. The last car is the caboose. Some people even sleep in beds on a train! A car has four wheels. Most people have a car. A car rides on roads. A bus can hold many people. A bus rides on roads. Most children ride a bus to school.

1. A boat floats on the _____.

2. If you want to get somewhere fast, which transportation would you use?

_____

3. The first car on a train is called an engine and the

last car is a _____.

4. _____ ride on a bus.

5. A _____ has four wheels.

Dairy Delights

Directions: Read the story. Answer the questions. Try the recipe.

Cows Give Us Milk

Cows live on a farm. The farmer milks the cows to get the milk. Many things are made from milk. We make ice cream, sour cream, cottage cheese and butter from milk. Butter is fun to make! You can learn to make your own butter. First, you need cream. Put the cream in a jar and shake it. Then, you need to pour off the liquid. Next, you put the butter in a bowl. Add a little salt and stir! Finally, spread it on crackers and eat!

1. What animal gives us milk?_____

2. What 4 things are made from milk?

   _____   _____

   _____   _____

3. What did the story teach you to make?_____

4. Put the steps in order. Place 1, 2, 3, 4 by the sentence.

   _____ Spread the butter on crackers and eat!

   _____ Shake cream in a jar.

   _____ Start with cream.

   _____ Add salt to the butter.

Get the Story Straight

Spencer likes to make new friends. Today, he made friends with the dog in the picture.

Directions: Number the sentences in order to find out what Spencer did today.

_____ Spencer kissed his mother good-bye.

_____ Spencer saw the new dog next door.

_____ Spencer went outside.

_____ Spencer said hello.

_____ Spencer got dressed and ate breakfast.

_____ Spencer woke up.

Snacktime!

Alana and Marcus are hungry for a snack. They want to make nacho chips and cheese. The steps they need to follow are all mixed up.

Directions: Read the steps. Number them in 1, 2, 3 order. Then, color the picture.

_____ Bake the chips in the oven for 2 minutes.

_____ Get a cookie sheet to bake on.

_____ Get out the nacho chips and cheese.

_____ Eat the nachos and chips.

_____ Put the chips on the cookie sheet.

_____ Put grated cheese on the chips.

Rain, Rain, Go Away

Directions: Read about rain. Then, follow the instructions.

Clouds are made up of little drops of ice and water. They push and bang into each other. Then, they join together to make bigger drops and begin to fall. More raindrops cling to them. They become heavy and fall quickly to the ground.

Write **first**, **second**, **third**, **fourth** and **fifth** to put the events in order.

_____ More raindrops cling to them.

_____ Clouds are made up of little drops of ice and water.

_____ They join together and make bigger drops that begin to fall.

_____ The drops of ice and water bang into each other.

_____ The drops become heavy and fall quickly to the ground.

Follow Me

Directions: Read the sentences. Follow the instructions.

1. On Monday, Lisa needs bread. Use a **red** crayon to mark her path from her house to that building.

   Where does she go? _____

2. On Tuesday, Lisa wants to read books. Use a **green** crayon to mark her path.

   Where does she go? _____

3. On Wednesday, Lisa wants to swing. Use a **yellow** crayon to mark her path.

   Where does she go? _____

4. On Thursday, Lisa wants to buy stamps. Use a **black** crayon to mark her path.

   Where does she go? _____

5. On Friday, Lisa wants to get money. Use a **purple** crayon to mark her path.

   Where does she go? _____

Map It!

Directions: Study the map of the United States. Follow the instructions.

1. Draw a star on the state where you live.

2. Draw a line from your state to the Atlantic Ocean.

3. Draw a triangle in the Gulf of Mexico.

4. Draw a circle in the Pacific Ocean.

5. Color each state that borders your state a different color.

CANADA

Pacific Ocean

Atlantic Ocean

Gulf of Mexico

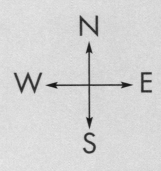

N

W   E

S

Dare to Be Different

Directions: Look at the pictures. Draw an **X** on the picture in each row that is different.

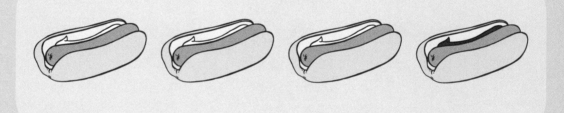

Birds of a Feather

Directions: Read about parrots and bluebirds. Then, complete the Venn diagram, telling how they are the same and different.

Bluebirds and parrots are both birds. Bluebirds and parrots can fly. They both have beaks. Parrots can live inside a cage. Bluebirds must live outdoors.

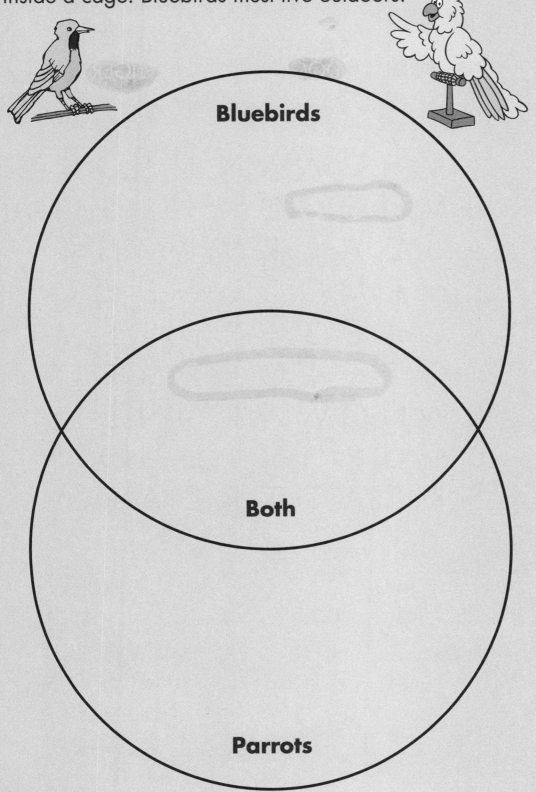

Bluebirds

Both

Parrots

READING

62

Classifying Critters

Directions: Use a **red** crayon to circle the names of three animals that would make good pets. Use a **blue** crayon to circle the names of three wild animals. Use an **orange** crayon to circle the two animals that live on a farm.

BEAR	CAT	LION	SHEEP
BIRD	▬▬	COW	▬▬

```
A M E O W W N L I O N
B M O D O G G X I I S O
A B E A R R V L M H R
R M R M O O U S E E K
K C A B B I R D S E M
I O T T I G E R M P Q
B W N O W W R Q N E N
D N C P H H I D U D N
F K C A T T R O A R M
```

Rainy Day Play

Directions: Read the story. Then, circle the objects Jonathan needs to stay dry.

It is raining. Jonathan wants to play outdoors. What should he wear to stay dry? What should he carry to stay dry?

Art Smart

Directions: Read about art tools. Then, color only the art tools.

Andrea uses different art tools to help her design her masterpieces. To cut, she needs scissors. To draw, she needs a pencil. To color, she needs crayons. To paint, she needs a brush.

Write which tools are needed to:

draw   color   cut

_____   _____   _____

Super Groups

Directions: The words in each box form a group. Choose the word from the word box that describes each group and write it on the line.

clothes	family	noises	colors	flowers
fruits	animals	coins	toys	

rose
buttercup
tulip
daisy

_____

crash
bang
ring
pop

_____

mother
father
sister
brother

_____

puzzle
wagon
blocks
doll

_____

green
purple
blue
red

_____

grapes
orange
apple
plum

_____

shirt
socks
dress
coat

_____

dime
penny
nickel
quarter

_____

dog
horse
elephant
moose

_____

Tricky Tree

This tricky tree has four different kinds of leaves: ash, poison ivy, silver maple and white oak.

Directions: Follow the instructions. Then, answer the questions.

1. Underline the white oak leaves.

    How many are there? _____

2. Circle the ash leaves.

    How many are there? _____

3. Draw an **X** on the poison ivy leaves.

    How many are there? _____

4. Draw a box around the silver maple leaves.

    How many are there? _____

A Look at Ladybugs

Directions: Read about ladybugs. Then, answer the questions.

Have you ever seen a ladybug? Ladybugs are red. They have black spots. They have six legs. Ladybugs are pretty!

1. What color are ladybugs? _____

2. What color are their spots? _____

3. How many legs do ladybugs have? _____

Paper Puppets

Directions: Read about paper-bag puppets. Then, follow the instructions.

It is easy to make a hand puppet. You need a small paper bag. You need colored paper. You need glue. You need scissors. Are you ready?

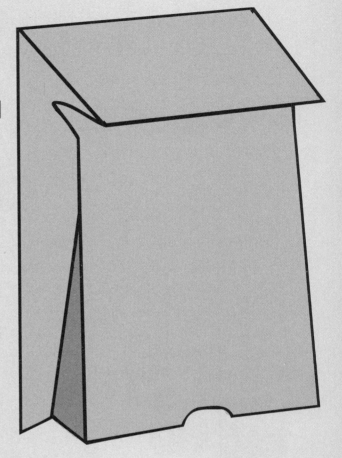

1. Circle the main idea:

    You need scissors.

    Making a hand puppet is easy.

2. Write the four objects you need to make a paper-bag puppet.

    1) _____

    2) _____

    3) _____

    4) _____

3. Draw a face on the paper-bag puppet.

Nice to Meet You

Directions: Read about how to meet a dog. Then, follow the instructions.

Do not try to pet a dog right away. First, let the dog sniff your hand. Do not move quickly. Do not talk loudly. Just let the dog sniff.

1. Predict what the dog will let you do if it likes you.

   _____

   _____

2. What should you let the dog do? _____

   _____

3. Name three things you should not do when you meet a dog.

   1) _____

   2) _____

   3) _____

Sean Leads the Team

Directions: Read about Sean's basketball game. Then, answer the questions.

Sean really likes to play basketball. One sunny day, he decided to ask his friends to play basketball at the park, but there were six people—Sean, Aki, Lance, Kate, Zac and Oralia. A basketball team only allows five to play at a time. So, Sean decided to be the coach. Sean and his friends had fun.

1. How many kids wanted to play basketball? _____

2. Write their names in ABC order:

   _____

   _____

   _____

   _____

   _____

   _____

3. How many players can play on a basketball team

   at a time? _____

4. Where did they play basketball? _____

5. Who decided to be the coach? _____

Rained Out

Predicting is telling what is likely to happen based on the facts.

Directions: Read the story. Then, check each sentence below that tells how the story could end.

One cloudy day, Juan and his baseball team, the Bears, played the Crocodiles. It was the last half of the fifth inning, and it started to rain. The coaches and umpires had to decide what to do.

_____ They kept playing until nine innings were finished.

_____ They ran for cover and waited until the rain stopped.

_____ Each player grabbed an umbrella and returned to the field to finish the game.

_____ They canceled the game and played it another day.

_____ They acted like crocodiles and slid around the wet bases.

_____ The coaches played the game while the players sat in the dugout.

Dog-Gone!

Directions: Read the story. Then, follow the instructions.

Scotty and Simone were washing their dog, Willis. His fur was wet. Their hands were wet. Willis did NOT like to be wet. Scotty dropped the soap. Simone picked it up and let go of Willis. Uh-oh!

1. Write what happened next.

_____

_____

_____

2. Draw what happened next.

Game Time!

A **fact** is something that can be proven. An **opinion** is a feeling or belief about something and cannot be proven.

Directions: Read these sentences about different games. Then, write **F** next to each fact and **O** next to each opinion.

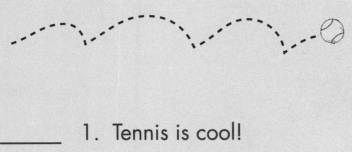

_____ 1. Tennis is cool!

_____ 2. There are red and black markers in a Checkers game.

_____ 3. In football, a touchdown is worth six points.

_____ 4. Being a goalie in soccer is easy.

_____ 5. A yo-yo moves on a string.

_____ 6. June's sister looks like the queen on the card.

_____ 7. The six kids need three more players for a baseball team.

_____ 8. Table tennis is more fun than court tennis.

Owls Are a Hoot

Directions: Read the story. Then, follow the instructions.

My name is Owen Owl, and I am a bird. I go to Nocturnal School. Our teacher is Mr. Screech Owl. In his class I learned that owls are birds and can sleep all day and hunt at night. Some of us live in nests in trees. In North America, it is against the law to harm owls. I like being an owl!

Write **F** next to each fact and **O** next to each opinion.

_____ 1. No one can harm owls in North America.

_____ 2. It would be great if owls could talk.

_____ 3. Owls sleep all day.

_____ 4. Some owls sleep in nests.

_____ 5. Mr. Screech Owl is a good teacher.

_____ 6. Owls are birds.

_____ 7. Owen Owl would be a good friend.

_____ 8. Owls hunt at night.

Chef Jeff

Directions: Read the story. Then, answer the questions.

Jeff is baking cookies. He wears special clothes when he bakes. He puts flour, sugar, eggs and butter into a bowl. He mixes everything together. He puts the cookies in the oven at 11:15 A.M. It takes 15 minutes for the cookies to bake. Jeff wants something cold and white to drink when he eats his cookies.

1. Is Jeff baking a cake?   Yes   No

2. What are two things that Jeff might wear when he bakes?

   hat   boots   apron   tie   raincoat   roller skates

3. What didn't Jeff put in the cookies?

   flour   eggs   milk   butter   sugar

4. What do you think Jeff does after he mixes the cookies but before he bakes them?

   _____

   _____

5. What time will the cookies be done? _____

6. What will Jeff drink with his cookies? _____

7. Why do you think Jeff wanted to bake cookies?

   _____

   _____

Mother's Helper

Directions: Read more about sea horses. Then, answer the questions.

A father sea horse helps the mother. He has a small sack or pouch, on the front of his body. The mother sea horse lays the eggs. She does not keep them. She gives the eggs to the father.

1. What does the mother sea horse do with her eggs?

   _____

2. Where does the father sea horse put the eggs?

   _____

3. Sea horses can change color. Color the sea horses.

What Do You See?

Directions: Read this story about Ling and Bradley. Draw pictures for the beginning and middle to describe each part of the story.

Beginning: One sunny day, Ling and Bradley, wearing their empty backpacks, rode their bikes down the street to the park.

Middle: They stopped by an oak tree with many acorns under it. They picked up some and stuffed them into their backpacks.

Directions: Draw an ending for this story that tells what you think they did with the acorns.

End: With the heavy backpacks strapped on their backs, they pedaled home.

It's No Problem!

Juniper has three problems to solve. She needs your help.

Directions: Read each problem. Write what you think she should do.

1. Juniper is watching her favorite TV show when the power goes out.

_____

_____

_____

_____

2. Juniper is riding her bike to school when the front tire goes flat.

_____

_____

_____

_____

3. Juniper loses her father while shopping in the supermarket.

_____

_____

_____

_____

Picture This

Directions: Draw three pictures to tell a story about each topic.

1. Feeding a pet

2. Playing with a friend

Beginning

Beginning

Middle

Middle

End

End

Bookworms

Directions: Use the clues to help the children find their books. Draw a line from each child's name to the correct book.

Brett   Aki   Lorenzo   Kate   Zac   Oralia

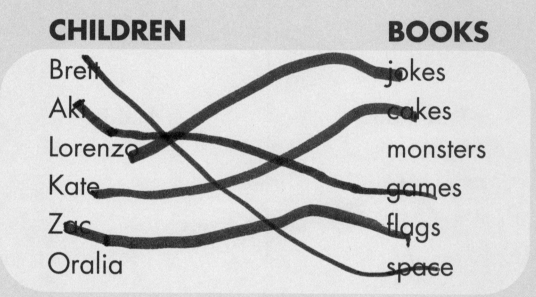

CHILDREN	BOOKS
Brett	jokes
Aki	cakes
Lorenzo	monsters
Kate	games
Zac	flags
Oralia	space

Clues

1. ~~Lorenzo likes space~~

2. ~~Kate likes to bake~~

3. Oralia likes far away places.

4. ~~Aki does not~~

6.

What's for Dinner?

Dad is cooking dinner tonight. You can find out what day of the week it is.

Directions: Read the clues. Complete the menu. Answer the question.

Menu

Monday _____

Tuesday _____

Wednesday _____

Thursday _____

Friday_____

Saturday _____

Sunday_____

1. Mom fixed pizza on Monday.

2. Dad fixed cheese rolls the day before that.

3. Tess made meat pie three days after Mom fixed pizza.

4. Tom fixed corn-on-the-cob the day before Tess made meat pie.

5. Mom fixed hot dogs the day after Tess made meat pie.

6. Tess cooked fish the day before Dad fixed cheese rolls.

7. Dad is making chicken today. What day is it?

_____

Review

Directions: Read the story. Then, answer the questions.

Randa, Emily, Ali, Dave, Liesl and Deana all love to read. Every Tuesday, they all go to the library together and pick out their favorite books. Randa likes books about fish. Emily likes books about sports and athletes. Ali likes books about art. Dave likes books about wild animals. Liesl likes books with riddles and puzzles. Deanna likes books about cats and dogs.

1. Circle the main idea:

   Randa, Emily, Ali, Dave, Liesl and Deana are good friends.

   Randa, Emily, Ali, Dave, Liesl and Deana all like books.

2. Who do you think might grow up to be an artist?

   _____

3. Who do you think might grow up to be an oceanographer (someone who studies the ocean)?

   _____

4. Who do you think might grow up to be a veterinarian (an animal doctor)?

   _____

5. Who do you think might grow up to be a zookeeper (someone who cares for zoo animals)?

   _____

Twister Tips

Directions: Read about tornadoes. Then, follow the instructions.

A tornado begins over land with strong winds and thunderstorms. The spinning air becomes a funnel. It can cause damage. If you are inside, go to the lowest floor of the building. A basement is a safe place. A bathroom or closet in the middle of a building can be a safe place, too. If you are outside, lie in a ditch. Remember, tornadoes are dangerous.

Write five facts about tornadoes.

1. _____

   _____

2. _____

   _____

3. _____

   _____

4. _____

   _____

5. _____

   _____

What a Breeze!

The setting is where a story takes place. The characters are the people in a story or play.

Directions: Read about Hercules. Then, answer the questions.

Hercules was born in the warm Atlantic Ocean. He was a very small and weak baby. He wanted to be the strongest hurricane in the world. But he had one problem. He couldn't blow 75-mile-per-hour winds. Hercules blew and blew in the ocean, until one day, his sister, Hola, told him it would be more fun to be a breeze than a hurricane. Hercules agreed. It was a breeze to be a breeze!

1. What is the setting of the story?

_____

2. Who are the characters?

_____

3. What is the problem?

_____

4. How does Hercules solve his problem?

_____

_____

Red, White, and Blue

Directions: Read each story. Then, write whether it is fiction or nonfiction.

One sunny day in July, a dog named Stan ran away from home. He went up one street and down the other looking for fun, but all the yards were empty. Where was everybody? Stan kept walking until he heard the sound of band music and happy people. Stan walked faster until he got to Central Street. There he saw men, women, children and dogs getting ready to walk in a parade. It was the Fourth of July!

Fiction or Nonfiction? _____

Americans celebrate the Fourth of July every year, because it is the birthday of the United States of America. On July 4, 1776, the United States got its independence from Great Britain. Today, Americans celebrate this holiday with parades, picnics and fireworks as they proudly wave the red, white and blue American flag.

Fiction or Nonfiction? _____

Hisssss!

Directions: Write a fictional (make-believe) story about a snake. Make sure to include details and a title.

_____ title

_____

_____

_____

_____

_____

_____

_____

_____

_____

_____

_____

English

Know Your ABCs

Directions: Write these words in order. If two words start with the same letter, look at the second letter in each word.

Example: lamb   Lamb comes first because **a** comes
         light   before **i** in the alphabet.

tree   _____

branch _____

leaf   _____

dish   _____

dog   _____

bone   _____

rain   _____

umbrella _____

cloud   _____

mail   _____

stamp   _____

slot   _____

From A to Z

If the first letters of two words are the same, look at the second letters in both words. If the second letters are the same, look at the third letters.

Directions: Write 1, 2, 3 or 4 on the lines in each row to put the words in ABC order.

Example:

1. __1__ candy   __2__ carrot   __4__ duck   __3__ dance

2. __2__ cold   __4__ hot   __1__ carry   __3__ hit

3. __2__ flash   __1__ fan   __3__ fun   __4__ garden

4. __2__ seat   __4__ sun   __1__ saw   __3__ sit

5. __3__ row   __1__ ring   __2__ rock   __4__ run

6. __2__ truck   __3__ turn   __4__ twin   __1__ talk

Friends and Family

Directions: Write the following names in ABC order: Oscar, Ali, Lance, Kim, Zane and Bonita.

_____

_____

_____

_____

_____

_____

Directions: Write the names of six of your friends or family in ABC order.

_____

_____

_____

_____

_____

_____

Super Similar

Words that mean the same or nearly the same are called **synonyms**.

Directions: Read the sentence that tells about the picture. Draw a circle around the word that means the same as the **bold** word.

The child is **unhappy**.

 hungry

The flowers are **lovely**.

 green

The baby was very **tired**.

 hurt

The **funny** clown made us laugh.

 glad

The ladybug is so **tiny**.

 red

We saw a **scary** tiger.

 ugly

A Silly Synonym Story

Synonyms are words that have almost the same meaning.

Directions: Read the story. Then, fill in the blanks with the synonyms.

| funny | unhappy |
| windy | little |

A New Balloon

It was a breezy day. The wind blew the small child's balloon away. The child was sad. A silly clown gave him a new balloon.

1. It was a _____ day.

2. The wind blew the _____ child's balloon away.

3. The child was _____.

4. A _____ clown gave him a new balloon.

So Many Synonyms!

Directions: Read each sentence. Fill in the blanks with the synonyms.

| friend | tired | story | presents | little |

I want to go to bed because I am very <u>sleepy</u>.

_____

On my birthday I like to open my <u>gifts</u>.

_____

My <u>pal</u> and I like to play together.

_____

My favorite <u>tale</u> is *Cinderella*.

_____

The mouse was so <u>tiny</u> that it was hard to catch him.

_____

All About Antonyms

Antonyms are words that mean the opposite of another word.

Examples:

hot and **cold**
short and **tall**

Directions: Draw a line from each word on the left to its antonym on the right.

sad	white
bottom	stop
black	fat
tall	top
thin	hard
little	found
cold	short
lost	hot
go	big
soft	happy

Spotty on the Go

Directions: Read the sentences. Complete each sentence with the correct antonym. Use the clues in the picture and below each sentence. Then, color the picture.

1. Spotty's suitcase is ____ .
   (antonym for closed)

   _____

2. Spotty has a ____ on his face.
   (antonym for frown)

   _____

3. His pillow is ____ .
   (antonym for hard)

   _____

4. His coat is ____ .
   (antonym for little)

   _____

5. Spotty packs his stuffed animal ____ .
   (antonym for first)

   _____

Hearing Homophones

Homophones are words that sound the same but are spelled differently and mean different things.

Directions: Write the homophone from the box next to each picture.

blew

sew _____ so

pair _____ pear

sea _____ see

blue _____ blew

Which One's Which?

Directions: Look at each picture. Circle the correct homophone.

(deer)   dear   blue   (blew)

(two)   to   hi   (high)

by   (bye)   (new)   knew

Nouns I Know

A noun is the name of a person, place or thing.

Directions: Read the story and circle all the nouns. Then, write the nouns next to the pictures below.

Our family likes to go to the park.

_____

_____

We play on the swings.

_____

We eat cake.

_____

We drink lemonade.

_____

We throw the ball to our dog.

_____

_____

Then, we go home.

_____

Nouns All Around

Directions: Look through a magazine. Cut out pictures of nouns and glue them below. Write the name of the noun next to the picture.

Nouns

Name-It Nouns

Proper nouns are the names of specific people, places and pets. Proper nouns begin with a capital letter.

Directions: Write the proper nouns on the lines below. Use capital letters at the beginning of each word.

logan, utah

_____

mike smith

_____

lynn cramer

_____

buster

_____

fluffy

_____

chicago, illinois

_____

It's a Date!

The days of the week and the months of the year are always capitalized.

Directions: Circle the words that are written correctly. Write the words that need capital letters on the lines below.

sunday	July	Wednesday
may	december	friday
tuesday	june	august
Monday	january	February
March	Thursday	April
September	saturday	October

Days of the Week   **Months of the Year**

1. _____   1. _____

2. _____   2. _____

3. _____   3. _____

4. _____   4. _____

                              5. _____

A Capital Idea

The first word and all of the important words in a title begin with a capital letter.

Directions: Write the book titles on the lines below. Use capital letters.

1. _____

2. _____

3. _____

4. _____

5. _____

6. _____

A Number of Nouns

Plural nouns name more than one person, place or thing.

Directions: Read the words in the box. Write the words in the correct column.

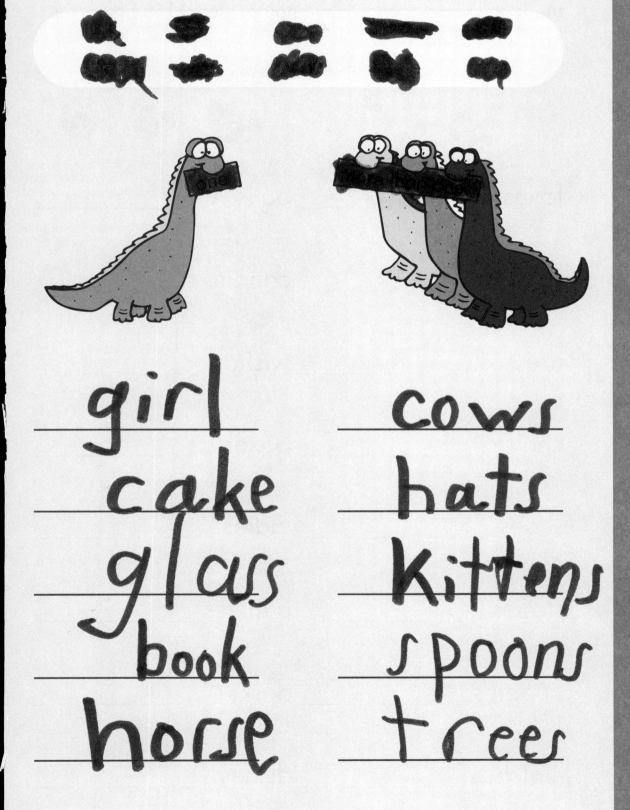

girl	cows
cake	hats
glass	kittens
book	spoons
horse	trees

Plenty of Plurals

Plurals are words that mean more than one. You usually add an **s** or **es** to the word. In some words ending in **y**, the **y** changes to an **i** before adding **es**. For example, **baby** changes to **babies**.

Directions: Look at the following lists of plural words. Write the word that means one next to it. The first one has been done for you.

foxes	<u>fox</u>	balls	_____
bushes	_____	candies	_____
dresses	_____	wishes	_____
chairs	_____	boxes	_____
shoes	_____	ladies	_____
stories	_____	bunnies	_____
puppies	_____	desks	_____
matches	_____	dishes	_____

Pronoun Pros

Pronouns are words that can be used instead of nouns. **She**, **he**, **it** and **they** are pronouns.

Directions: Read the sentence. Then, write the sentence again, using **she**, **he**, **it** or **they** in the blank.

1. Dan likes funny jokes.

   _____ likes funny jokes.

2. Peg and Sam went to the zoo.

   _____ went to the zoo.

3. My dog likes to dig in the yard.

   _____ likes to dig in the yard.

4. Sara is a very good dancer.

   _____ is a very good dancer.

5. Fred and Ted are twins.

   _____ are twins.

What's It All About?

The **subject** of a sentence is the person, place or thing the sentence is about.

Directions: Underline the subject in each sentence.

Example: Mom read a book.
(Think: Who is the sentence about? <u>Mom</u>)

1. The bird flew away.

2. The kite was high in the air.

3. The children played a game.

4. The books fell down.

5. The monkey climbed a tree.

Double Up

Two similar sentences can be joined into one sentence if the predicate is the same. A **compound subject** is made up of two subjects joined together by the word **and**.

Example: Jamie can sing.
Sandy can sing.

Jamie **and** Sandy can sing.

Directions: Combine the sentences. Write the new sentence on the line.

1. The cats are my pets.
The dogs are my pets.

_____

_____

2. Chairs are in the store.
Tables are in the store.

_____

_____

3. Tom can ride a bike.
Jack can ride a bike.

_____

_____

Play Ball!

A **verb** is the action word in a sentence. Verbs tell what something does or that something exists.

Example: Run, **sleep** and **jump** are verbs.

Directions: Circle the verbs in the sentences below.

1. We play baseball everyday.

2. Susan pitches the ball very well.

3. Mike swings the bat harder than anyone.

4. Chris slides into home base.

5. Laura hit a home run.

Verb Alert!

We use verbs to tell when something happens. Sometimes we add an **ed** to verbs that tell us if something has already happened.

Example: Today, we will **play**. Yesterday, we **played**.

Directions: Write the correct verb in the blank.

1. Today, I will _____ my dog, Fritz.
   wash   washed

2. Last week, Fritz _____ when we
   cry   cried

   said, "Bath time, Fritz."

3. My sister likes to _____ wash Fritz.
   help   helped

4. One time she _____ Fritz
   by herself.   clean   cleaned

5. Fritz will _____ a lot better after
   his bath.   look   looked

Predicate Power

The **predicate** is the part of the sentence that tells about the action.

Directions: Circle the predicate in each sentence.

Example: The boys ran on the playground.

(Think: The boys did what? (Ran))

1. The woman painted a picture.

2. The puppy chases his ball.

3. The students went to school.

4. Butterflies fly in the air.

5. The baby wants a drink.

Twice the Action

A **compound predicate** is made by joining two sentences that have the same subject. The predicates are joined together by the word **and**.

Example: Tom can jump.

Tom can run.

Tom can run **and** jump.

Directions: Combine the sentences. Write the new sentence on the line.

1. The dog can roll over.
   The dog can bark.

_____

_____

2. My mom plays with me.
   My mom reads with me.

_____

_____

3. Tara is tall.
   Tara is smart.

_____

_____

School Days

The **subject** part of the sentence is the person, place or thing the sentence is about. The **predicate** is the part of the sentence that tells what the subject does.

Directions: Draw a line between the subject and the predicate. Underline the noun in the subject and circle the verb.

Example: The furry <u>cat</u> | (ate) food.

1. Mandi walks to school.

2. The bus drove the children.

3. The school bell rang very loudly.

4. The teacher spoke to the students.

5. The girls opened their books.

All Together Now

Directions: Write one new sentence using a compound subject or predicate.

Example: The boy will jump. The girl will jump.

The <u>boy and girl</u> will jump.

1. The clowns run. The clowns play.

_____

_____

2. The dogs dance. The bears dance.

_____

_____

3. Seals bark. Seals clap.

_____

_____

4. The girls play. The girls laugh.

_____

_____

Ready to Roll

Directions: Draw a circle around the noun, the naming part of the sentence. Draw a line under the verb, the action part of the sentence.

Example: (John) <u>drinks</u> juice every morning.

1. Our class skates at the roller-skating rink.

2. Miguel and Emma go very fast.

3. Austin eats hot dogs.

4. Sierra dances to the music.

5. Everyone likes the skating rink.

Tell Me More!

Adjectives are words that tell more about a person, place or thing.

Examples: cold, fuzzy, dark

Directions: Circle the adjectives in the sentences.

1. The juicy apple is on the plate.

2. The furry dog is eating a bone.

3. It was a sunny day.

4. The kitten drinks warm milk.

5. The baby has a loud cry.

A Day on the Farm

Directions: Choose an adjective from the box to fill in the blanks.

hungry	sunny	busy	funny
fresh	deep	pretty	cloudy

1. It is a _____ day on Farmer Brown's farm.

2. Farmer Brown is a very _____ man.

3. Mrs. Brown likes to feed the _____ chickens.

4. Every day she collects the _____ eggs.

5. The ducks swim in the _____ pond.

Make a Wish!

Articles are small words that help us to better understand nouns. **A** and **an** are articles. We use **an** before a word that begins with a vowel. We use a before **a** word that begins with a consonant.

Example: We looked in **a** nest. It had **an** eagle in it.

Directions: Read the sentences. Write **a** or **an** in the blank.

1. 1. I found _____ book.

2. It had a story about _____ ant in it.

3. In the story, _____ lion gave three wishes to ant.

4. The ant's first wish was to ride _____ elephant.

5. The second wish was to ride _____ alligator.

6. The last wish was _____ wish for three more wishes.

Sentence Sense

A **sentence** tells a complete idea. It has a noun and a verb. It begins with a capital letter and has punctuation at the end.

Directions: Circle the group of words if it is a sentence.

1. Grass is a green plant.

2. Mowing the lawn.

3. Grass grows in fields and lawns.

4. Tickle the feet.

5. Sheep, cows and horses eat grass.

6. We like to play in.

7. My sister likes to mow the lawn.

8. A picnic on the grass.

Making a Statement

Statements are sentences that tell us something. They begin with a capital letter and end with a period.

Directions: Write the sentences on the lines below. Begin each sentence with a capital letter and end it with a period.

1. we like to ride our bikes

_____

_____

2. we go down the hill very fast

_____

_____

3. we keep our bikes shiny and clean

_____

_____

4. we know how to change the tires

_____

Ask Me a Question

Questions are sentences that ask something. They begin with a capital letter and end with a question mark.

Directions: Write the questions on the lines below. Begin each sentence with a capital letter and end it with a question mark.

1. will you be my friend

_____

_____

2. what is your name

_____

_____

3. are you eight years old

_____

_____

4. do you like rainbows

_____

_____

What a Surprise!

Surprising sentences tell a strong feeling and end with an exclamation point. A surprising sentence may be only one or two words showing fear, surprise or pain.
Example: Oh, no!

Directions: Put a period at the end of the sentences that tell something. Put an exclamation point at the end of the sentences that tell a strong feeling. Put a question mark at the end of the sentences that ask a question.

1. The cheetah can run very fast

2. Wow

3. Look at that cheetah go

4. Can you run fast

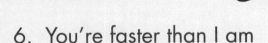

5. Oh, my

6. You're faster than I am

7. Let's run together

8. We can run as fast as a cheetah

9. What fun

10. Do you think cheetahs get tired

That's Mine!

We add **'s** to nouns (people, places or things) to tell who or what owns something.

Directions: Read the sentences. Fill in the blanks to show ownership.

Example: The doll belongs to **Sara**.

It is **Sara's** doll.

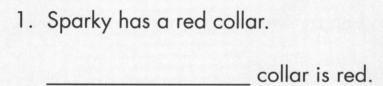

1. Sparky has a red collar.

   _____ collar is red.

2. Jimmy has a blue coat.

   _____ coat is blue.

3. The tail of the cat is short.

   The _____ tail is short.

4. The name of my mother is Karen.

   My _____ name is Karen.

Owning Up

Directions: Read the sentences. Choose the correct word and write it in the sentences below.

1. The _____ lunchbox is broken.

     boys   boy's

2. The _____ played in the cage.

     gerbil's   gerbils

3. _____ hair is brown.

     Anns   Ann's

4. The _____ ran in the field.

     horse's   horses

5. My _____ coat is torn.

     sister's   sisters

6. The _____ fur is brown.

     cats   cat's

7. Three _____ flew past our window.

     birds   bird's

8. The _____ paws are muddy.

     dogs   dog's

Look It Up

A dictionary is a book that gives the meaning of words. It also tells how words sound. Words in a dictionary are in ABC order. That makes them easier to find. A picture dictionary lists a word, a picture of the word and its meaning.

Directions: Look at this page from a picture dictionary. Then, answer the questions.

baby

A very young child.

band

A group of people who play music.

bank

A place where money is kept.

bark

The sound a dog makes.

berry

A small, juicy fruit.

board

A flat piece of wood.

1. What is a small, juicy fruit? _____

2. What is a group of people who play music? _____

3. What is the name for a very young child? _____

4. What is a flat piece of wood called? _____

Word to Word

The guide words at the top of a page in a dictionary tell you what the first and last words on the page will be. Only words that come in ABC order between those two words will be on that page. Guide words help you find the page you need to look up a word.

Directions: Write each word from the box in ABC order between each pair of guide words.

faint	far	fence	feed	farmer
fan	feet	farm	family	face

face   **fence**

_____   _____

_____   _____

_____   _____

_____   _____

_____   _____

Many Meanings

When words have more than one meaning, the meanings are numbered in a dictionary.

Directions: Read the meanings of **tag**. Write the number of the correct definition after each sentence.

tag

1. A small strip or tab attached to something else.

2. To label.

3. To follow closely and constantly.

4. A game of chase.

1. We will play a game of tag after we study. _____

2. I will tag this coat with its price. _____

3. My little brother will tag along with us. _____

4. My mother already took off the price tag. _____

5. The tag on the puppy said, "For Sale." _____

6. Do not tag that tree. _____

Spelling

Number Names

Directions: Write each number word beside the correct picture. Then, write it again.

Example:

six   six

one two three four five six seven eight nine ten

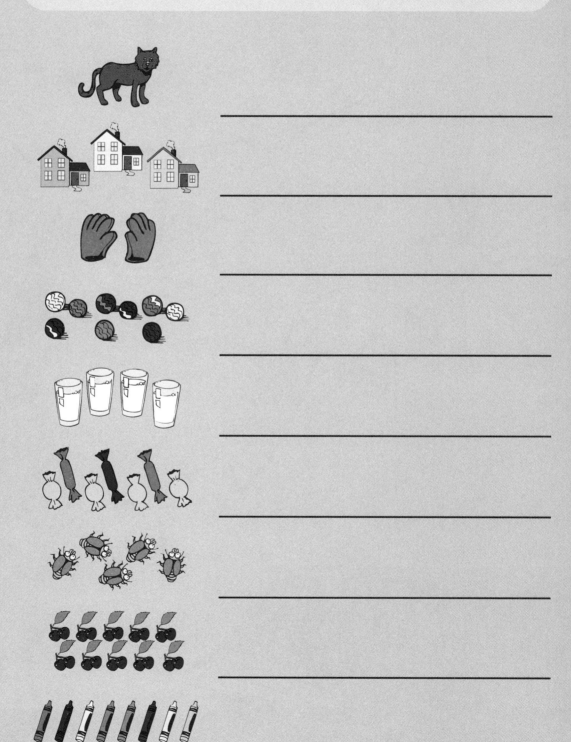

_____

_____

_____

_____

_____

_____

_____

_____

_____

Say It With Numbers

Directions: Change the telling sentences into asking sentences. Change the asking sentences into telling sentences. Begin each one with a capital letter and end it with a period or a question mark.

Examples:

Is she eating three cookies?

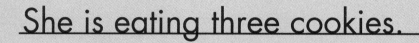

She is eating three cookies.

He is bringing one truck.

Is he bringing one truck?

1. Is he painting two bluebirds?

   _____

   _____

2. Did she find four apples?

   _____

   _____

3. She will be six on her birthday.

   _____

   _____

Super Sounds: Short a

Directions: Use a word from the box to complete each sentence.

fat	path	lamp	can
van	stamp	Dan	math
sat	cat	fan	bat

Example:

1. The _____lamp_____ had a pink shade.

2. The bike _____ led us to the park.

3. I like to add in _____ class.

4. The cat is very _____.

5. The _____ of beans was hard to open.

6. The envelope needed a _____.

7. He swung the _____ and hit the ball.

8. The _____ blew air around.

9. My mom drives a blue _____.

10. I _____ in the backseat.

Super Sounds: Long a

Long a is the vowel sound which says its own name.
Long a can be spelled **ai** as in the word **mail**, **ay** as
in the word **say** and **a** with a **silent e** at the end of a
word as in the word **same**.

Directions: Say each word and listen for the **long a**
sound. Then, write each word and underline the letters
that make the **long a** vowel sound.

mail	bake	train
game	day	sale
paint	play	name
made	gray	tray

1. _____

2. _____

3. _____

4. _____

5. _____

6. _____

7. _____

8. _____

9. _____

10. _____

11. _____

12. _____

Super Sounds: Short e

Directions: Write the correct short e word in each sentence.

get	Meg	rest	bed	spent
test	head	pet	red	best

1. Of all my crayons, I like the _____

   color the _____!

2. I always make my _____ when I

   _____ up.

3. My new hat keeps my _____
   warm.

4. _____ wanted a dog

   for a _____.

5. I have a _____ in math tomorrow,

   so I want to get a good night's _____.

Super Sounds: Long e

Long e is the vowel sound which says its own name. **Long e** can be spelled **ee** as in the word **teeth**, **ea** as in the word **meat** or **e** as in the word **me**.

Directions: Say each word and listen for the **long e** sound. Then, write the words and underline the letters that make the **long e** sound.

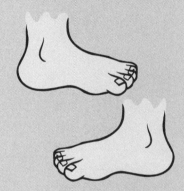

street	neat	treat
feet	sleep	keep
deal	meal	mean
clean	beast	feast

1. _____

2. _____

3. _____

4. _____

5. _____

6. _____

7. _____

8. _____

9. _____

10. _____

11. _____

12. _____

Super Sounds: Short i

Short i is the sound you hear in the word **pin**.

Directions: Use the **short i** words in the box to write rhyming words.

pin	fin	win	fish
pitch	wish	rich	kick
ship	dip	dish	sick

1. Write the words that rhyme with **spin**.

   _____ _____ _____

2. Write the words that rhyme with **ditch**.

   _____ _____

3. Write the words that rhyme with **rip**.

   _____ _____

4. Write the words that rhyme with **squish**.

   _____ _____ _____

5. Write the words that rhyme with **lick**.

   _____ _____

Super Sounds: Long i

Long i is the vowel sound which says its own name. **Long i** can be spelled **igh** as in **sight**, **i** with a **silent e** at the end as in **mine** and **y** at the end as in **fly**.

Directions: Say each word and listen for the **long i** sound. Then, write each word and underline the letters that make the **long i** sound.

bike	hike	ride
line	glide	ripe
nine	pipe	fight
high	light	sigh

1. _____

2. _____

3. _____

4. _____

5. _____

6. _____

7. _____

8. _____

9. _____

10. _____

11. _____

12. _____

Super Sounds: Short o

Short o is the vowel sound you hear in the word **got**.

Directions: Use the **short o** words in the box to write rhyming words.

hot	rock
lock	cot
stop	sock
fox	mop
box	clock

1. Write the words that rhyme with **dot**.

   _____   _____

2. Write the words that rhyme with **socks**.

   _____   _____

3. Write the words that rhyme with **hop**.

   _____   _____

4. Write the words that rhyme with **dock**.

   _____   _____

   _____   _____

Super Sounds: Long o

Directions: Draw a line from the first part of the sentence to the part which completes the sentence.

1. Do you know   in the water.

2. The dog   was in the tree.

3. The boat floats   who wrote the note?

4. I hope the phone   has a bone.

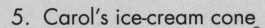

5. Carol's ice-cream cone   rings soon for me!

6. The rope swing   a coat in the cold.

7. I had to wear   was melting.

Super Sounds: Short u

Directions: Circle the words in each sentence which are not correct. Then, write the correct **short u** words from the box on the lines.

tub	cub	bump
pump	bug	dust
cut	must	nut
jump	rug	hug

1. The crust made me sneeze.

   _____

2. I need to take a bath in the cub.

   _____

3. The mug bite left a big pump on my arm.

   _____   _____

4. It is time to get my hair hut.

   _____

5. The mother bear took care of her shrub.

   _____

6. We need to jump more gas into the car.

   _____

Super Sounds: Long u

Long u is the vowel sound you hear in the word **cube**. Another vowel sound which is very much like the **long u** sound is the **oo** sound you hear in the word **boot**.

Directions: Use the **long u** and **oo** words in the box to write rhyming words.

moon	use	blew
flew	loose	choose
fuse	noon	goose

1. Write the words that rhyme with **soon**.

    _____ _____

2. Write the words that rhyme with **lose**.

    _____ _____ _____

3. Write the words that rhyme with **grew**.

    _____ _____

4. Write the words that rhyme with **moose**.

    _____ _____

Ready, Set, Action!

Verbs are words that tell the action in the sentence.

Directions: Draw a line from each sentence to its picture. Then, finish the sentence with the verb or action word that is under each picture.

Example:

He will _____ help _____ the baby.

carry

1. I can _____ my book.

help

2. It is time to _____ up.

cut

3. That chair might _____.

build

4. They _____ houses.

clean

5. I _____ this out myself.

fix

6. Is that too heavy to _____?

break

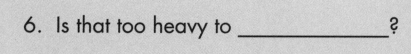

How Does It End?

Most **verbs** end with **s** when the sentence tells about one thing. The **s** is taken away when the sentence tells about more than one thing.

Example:

One dog walks.   One boy runs.
Two dogs **walk**.   Three boys **run**.

The spelling of some **verbs** changes when the sentence tells about only one thing.

One girl carries her lunch.   The boy fixes his car.
Two girls **carry** their lunches.   The boys **fix** their cars.

Directions: Write the missing verbs in the sentences.

Example:

Pam works hard. She and Peter _____work_____ all day.

1. The father bird builds a nest.

   The mother and father _____ it together.

2. The girls clean their room.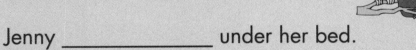

   Jenny _____ under her bed.

3. The children cut out their pictures.

   Henry _____ his slowly.

4. These workers fix things.

   This man _____ televisions.

5. Two trucks carry horses.

   One truck _____ pigs.

Animal Action

Directions: Circle the word in each sentence that is not spelled correctly. Then, write it correctly.

squirrel   bears   rabbit   deer   fox   mouse

Example:

Animals like to live in (threes.)   trees

1. Bares do not eat people.   _____

2. The squirel found a nut.   _____

3. Sometimes a little moose
    might get into your house.   _____

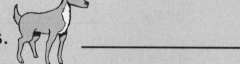

4. Dear eat leaves and grass.   _____

5. A focks has a bushy tail.   _____

6. One day, a rabitt came
    into our yard.   _____

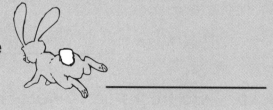

Lots of Animals

Directions: Write the two sentences below as one sentence. Remember the special spelling of **fox**, **mouse** and **deer** when there are more than one.

Example:

I saw a mouse. You saw a mouse.

<u>We saw two mice.</u>

1. Julie petted a deer.
   Matt petted a deer.

_____

_____

2. Mike colored a fox.
   Kim colored a fox.

_____

_____

All in the Family

Directions: This is Andy's **family tree**. It shows all the people in his family. Use the words in the box to finish writing the names in Andy's family tree.

grandmother   mother

grandfather   father

aunt   uncle

brother   sister

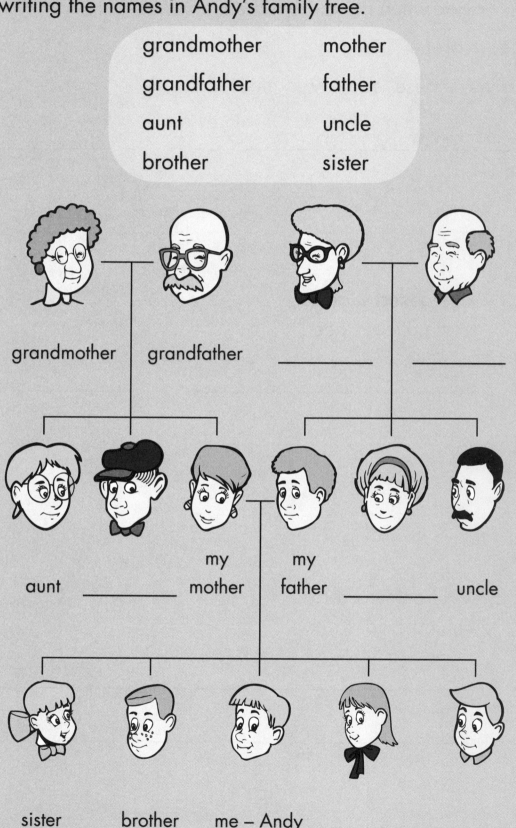

grandmother   grandfather   _____   _____

aunt   _____   my mother   my father   _____   uncle

sister   brother   me – Andy   _____   _____

Once Upon a Family

Directions: Write the family words in the blanks to complete the story.

One day, my family had a picnic. My

_____ baked chicken.

_____ baked some rolls.

My _____ Jack brought corn. My

_____ made something green and

white in a big dish. I ate the chicken my

_____ brought. I had two rolls made

by my _____. My _____

gave me some corn. I liked it all! Then, my

_____ and I looked in the dish my

_____ had brought. "Did you try it?"

I asked him.

"You're my big _____," he said.

"You try it!" I put a tiny bit in my mouth. It tasted good!

But the dish was almost empty.

"It's terrible!" I said. "I'll eat the rest of it so you

won't have to. That's what a big _____

is for!" My _____ watched me eat it all.

I tried not to look too happy!

Where in the World?

Directions: Draw a line from each sentence to its picture. Then, complete each sentence with the word under the picture.

Example:

He is walking ___behind___ the tree.

outside

1. We stay _____ when it rains.

behind

2. She drew a dog _____ his house.

between

3. She stands _____ her friends.

across

4. They walked _____ the bridge.

around

5. Let the cat go _____.

beside

6. Draw a circle _____ the fish.

inside

Find That Cat!

Directions: Use a location word to tell where the cat is in each sentence.

Example:

The cat is behind the box.

_____

_____

_____

_____

_____

_____

_____

_____

Heads or Tails?

Directions: Opposites are words which are different in every way. Use the opposite word from the box to complete these sentences.

hard	hot	bottom	quickly	happy
sad	slowly	cold	soft	top

Example:

My new coat is blue on _____**top**_____ and

red on the ___**bottom**___ .

1. Snow is _____, but fire is _____.

2. A rabbit runs _____, but a turtle

   moves _____.

3. A bed is _____, but a floor

   is _____.

4. I feel _____ when my friends come

   and _____ when they leave.

A Sweet Surprise

Directions: Write opposite words in the blanks to complete the story.

> hot   hard   top   cold   slowly
>
> soft   quickly   happy   bottom   sad

One day, Grandma came for a visit. She gave my sister Jenny and me a box of chocolate candy. We said, "Thank you!" Then, Jenny _____ took the _____ off the box. The pieces all looked the same! I couldn't tell which pieces were _____ inside and which were _____! I only liked the _____ ones. Jenny didn't care. She was _____ to get any kind of candy!

I _____ looked at all the pieces. I didn't know which one to pick. Just then Dad called us. Grandma was going home. He wanted us to say good-bye to her. I hurried to the front door where they were standing. Jenny came a minute later.

I told Grandma I hoped I would see her soon. I always feel _____ when she leaves. Jenny stood behind me and didn't say anything. After Grandma went home, I found out why. Jenny had most of our candy in her mouth! Only a few pieces were left in the _____ of the box! Then, I was _____! That Jenny!

Tick, Tock, Time

The time between breakfast and lunch is **morning**.

The time between lunch and dinner is **afternoon**.

The time between dinner and bedtime is **evening**.

Directions: Write a time word from the box to complete each sentence. Use each word only once.

evening   morning   today   tomorrow   afternoon

1. What did you eat for breakfast

   this _____?

2. We came home from school in

   the _____.

3. I help wash the dinner dishes in

   the _____.

4. I feel a little tired _____.

5. If I rest tonight, I will feel

   better _____.

What Time Is It?

Directions: Write a sentence for these time words. Tell something you do at that time.

Example:

day

<u>Every day I walk to school.</u>

morning

_____

_____

afternoon

_____

_____

evening

_____

_____

Review

Directions: Write the story below again and correct all the mistakes. Watch for words that are not spelled correctly, missing periods and question marks, question marks at the end of telling sentences and sentences with the wrong joining words.

One mourning, my granmother said I could have a pet mouse. That evenening, we got my mouse at the pet store, or the next afernoon my mouse had babies! Now, I had nyne mouses! I really liked to wach them? I wanted to pick the babies up, and they were too little. When they get bigger, I have to give too mouses to my sisster.

_____

_____

_____

_____

_____

_____

_____

_____

_____

_____

Math

Shape Escape!

Directions: Complete each row by drawing the correct shape.

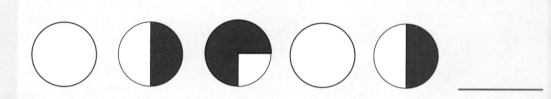

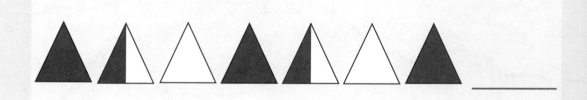

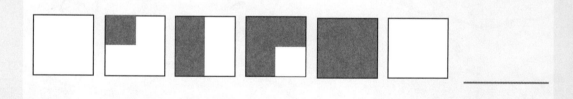

Pick a Pattern

Mia likes to count by twos, threes, fours, fives, tens and hundreds.

1   **2**   **3**   **4**   **5**

Directions: Complete the number patterns.

1. 5, **10**, **15**, 20, **25** **30** 35, **40** **45** 50

2. 100, **260** **300** 400, **500** **600** 700 800, **900**

3. **2**, 4, 6, **8**, **10** 12, **14**, 16, **18**, **20**

4. 10, **20**, **30** 40, **50** **60**, 70, **80** 90

5. 4, **8**, 12, **16** **20** 24, **28**, 32, **36** 40

Directions: Make up two of your own number patterns.

3, 6, 9, 12 15 18 21 24

50 100, 150 200 250 30° 35° 4°°

All Aboard!

Ordinal numbers indicate order in a series, such as **first**, **second** or **third**.

Directions: Follow the instructions to color the train cars. The first car is the engine.

Color the third car **blue**.

Color the eighth car **green**.

Color the fifth car **orange**.

Color the sixth car **yellow**.

Color the fourth car **brown**.

Color the second car **purple**.

Color the first car **red**.

Color the seventh car **pink**.

Add Attack!

Addition is "putting together" or adding two or more numbers to find the sum.

Directions: Add.

Example:

```
  2
+5
___
  7
```

```
  3        6        7        8        5
+4       +2       +1       +2       +4
___      ___      ___      ___      ___
  7        8        8       10        9
```

```
  8        9       10        6        4
+2       +5       +3       +6       +9
___      ___      ___      ___      ___
 10       14       13       12       13
```

```
  9        8        6        7        7
+3       +7       +5       +9       +6
___      ___      ___      ___      ___
 12       15       11       16       13
```

Add Attack: Forward and Back

The commutative property of addition states that even if the order of the numbers is changed in an addition sentence, the sum will stay tye same.

Example: 2 + 3 = 5
3 + 2 = 5

Directions: Look at the addition sentences below. Complete the addition sentences by writing the missing numerals.

5 + 4 = 9   3 + 1 = 4

4 + __ = 9   1 + __ = 4

2 + 6 = 8   6 + 1 = 7

6 + __ = 8   1 + __ = 7

Now try these:

6 + 3 = 9   10 + 2 = 12

__ + __ = 9   __ + __ = 12

Look at these sums. Can you think of two number sentences that would show the commutative property of addition.

__ + __ = 7   __ + __ = 11

__ + __ = 7   __ + __ = 11

Add Attack: 3 or More Numbers

Directions: Add all the numbers to find the sum. Draw pictures to help or break up the problem into two smaller problems.

Example:

$$
\begin{array}{r} 1 \\ 2 \\ +3 \\ \hline 6 \end{array}
$$

$$
\begin{array}{r} 2 \\ +5 \\ \hline \end{array} \Big\rangle \; 7
$$

$$
\begin{array}{r} 2 \\ +4 \\ \hline \end{array} \Big\rangle \; \begin{array}{r} +6 \\ \hline 13 \end{array}
$$

$$
\begin{array}{r} 3 \\ 6 \\ +2 \\ \hline \end{array}
\qquad
\begin{array}{r} 8 \\ 5 \\ +4 \\ \hline \end{array}
\qquad
\begin{array}{r} 3 \\ 1 \\ +5 \\ \hline \end{array}
\qquad
\begin{array}{r} 8 \\ 2 \\ +9 \\ \hline \end{array}
$$

$$
\begin{array}{r} 2 \\ 8 \\ 4 \\ +3 \\ \hline \end{array}
\qquad
\begin{array}{r} 3 \\ 6 \\ 5 \\ +2 \\ \hline \end{array}
\qquad
\begin{array}{r} 4 \\ 1 \\ 2 \\ +5 \\ \hline \end{array}
\qquad
\begin{array}{r} 6 \\ 7 \\ 3 \\ +1 \\ \hline \end{array}
$$

Take It Away!

Subtraction is "taking away" or subtracting one number from another to find the difference.

Directions: Subtract.

Example:

```
  4
 -3
 ___
  1
```

```
  5      6      4      3      2
 -3     -1     -3     -1     -0
 ___    ___    ___    ___    ___
  2      5      1      2      2
```

```
  9      7     10     14     15
 -2     -4     -5     -6     -9
 ___    ___    ___    ___    ___
  7      3      5      8      6
```

```
 18     13     14     11     17
 -8     -5     -7     -4     -9
 ___    ___    ___    ___    ___
 10      8      7      7      8
```

01-335141120

01-335141120

Find Your Place

The place value of a digit or numeral is shown by where it is in the number. For example, in the number **23**, **2** has the place value of **tens**, and **3** is **ones**.

Directions: Add the tens and ones and write your answers in the blanks.

Example:

🍌🍌🍌 🍌🍌🍌 🍌🍌🍌 + 🍌🍌🍌 = __33__

3 tens + 3 ones = __33__

tens ones   **tens ones**

7 tens + 5 ones = __75__   4 tens + 0 ones = __40__

2 tens + 3 ones = __23__   8 tens + 1 one = __81__

5 tens + 2 ones = __52__   1 ten + 1 one = __11__

5 tens + 4 ones = __54__   6 tens + 3 ones = __63__

Directions: Draw a line to the correct number.

6 tens + 7 ones   73

4 tens + 2 ones   67

8 tens + 0 ones   51

7 tens + 3 ones   80

5 tens + 1 one   42

Add Attack: 2 Digits

Directions: Study the example. Follow the steps to add.

Example:

$$\begin{array}{r} 33 \\ +41 \\ \hline \end{array}$$

Step 1: Add the ones.   **Step 2:** Add the tens.

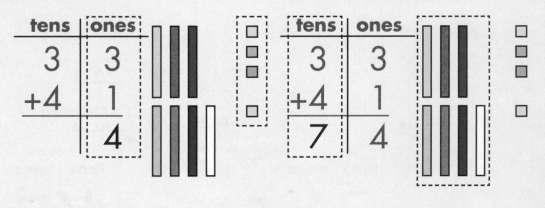

tens	ones
3	3
+4	1
	4

tens	ones
3	3
+4	1
7	4

tens	ones
4	2
+2	4
6	6

tens	ones
5	0
+4	7
9	7

$$\begin{array}{r} 24 \\ +62 \\ \hline \end{array} \qquad \begin{array}{r} 15 \\ +23 \\ \hline \end{array} \qquad \begin{array}{r} 38 \\ +61 \\ \hline \end{array} \qquad \begin{array}{r} 11 \\ +26 \\ \hline \end{array} \qquad \begin{array}{r} 37 \\ +42 \\ \hline \end{array}$$

$$\begin{array}{r} 25 \\ +42 \\ \hline \end{array} \qquad \begin{array}{r} 62 \\ +14 \\ \hline \end{array} \qquad \begin{array}{r} 32 \\ +44 \\ \hline \end{array} \qquad \begin{array}{r} 25 \\ +13 \\ \hline \end{array} \qquad \begin{array}{r} 82 \\ + 6 \\ \hline \end{array}$$

Add Attack: 2 Digits

Directions: Add the total points scored in each game. Remember to add **ones** first and **tens** second.

Example:

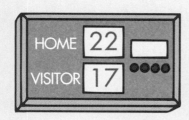

Total ___39___

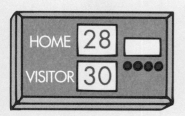

Total _____

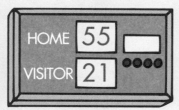

Total _____

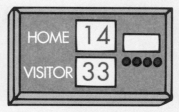

Total _____

Total _____

Total _____

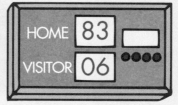

Total _____

Total _____

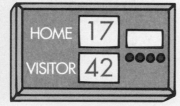

Total _____

Total _____

Add Attack: 2 Digits

Addition is "putting together" or adding two or more numbers to find the sum. Regrouping is using **ten ones** to form **one ten**, **ten tens** to form **one 100**, **fifteen ones** to form **one ten** and **five ones** and so on.

Directions: Study the examples. Follow the steps to add.

Example:

$$\begin{array}{r} 14 \\ +8 \\ \hline \end{array}$$

Step 1:
Add the ones.

Step 2:
Regroup the tens.

Step 3:
Add the tens.

tens	ones
1	
1	4
+	8
	12

tens	ones
1	
1	4
+	8
	2

tens	ones
1	
1	4
+	8
2	2

tens	ones
1	
1	6
+3	7
5	3

tens	ones
1	
3	8
+5	3
9	1

tens	ones
1	
2	4
+4	7
7	1

$$\begin{array}{r} 28 \\ +17 \\ \hline \end{array} \qquad \begin{array}{r} 32 \\ +38 \\ \hline \end{array} \qquad \begin{array}{r} 54 \\ +25 \\ \hline \end{array} \qquad \begin{array}{r} 19 \\ +55 \\ \hline \end{array} \qquad \begin{array}{r} 44 \\ +48 \\ \hline \end{array}$$

Add Attack: 2 Digits

Directions: Add the total points scored in the game. Remember to add the ones, regroup, and then add the tens.

Example:

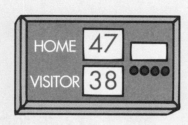

Total _____85_____

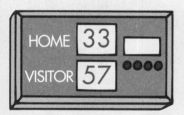

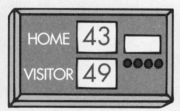

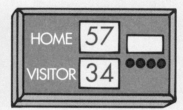

Total _____   Total _____   Total _____

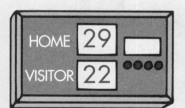

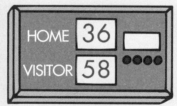

Total _____   Total _____   Total _____

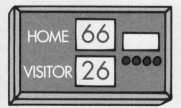

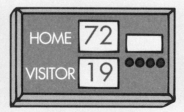

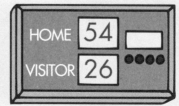

Total _____   Total _____   Total _____

Take It Away: 2 Digits

Directions: Study the example. Follow the steps to subtract.

Example:

$$
\begin{array}{r}
28 \\
-14 \\
\hline
\end{array}
$$

Step 1: Subtract the ones.   **Step 2:** Subtract the tens.

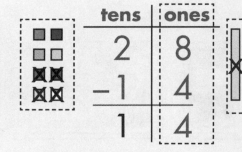

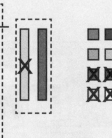

tens	ones		tens	ones
2	8		2	8
−1	4		−1	4
	4		1	4

tens	ones		tens	ones
2	4		3	8
−1	2		−1	5
1	2		2	3

$$
\begin{array}{r} 24 \\ -12 \\ \hline \end{array}
\qquad
\begin{array}{r} 61 \\ -30 \\ \hline \end{array}
\qquad
\begin{array}{r} 77 \\ -44 \\ \hline \end{array}
\qquad
\begin{array}{r} 85 \\ -24 \\ \hline \end{array}
\qquad
\begin{array}{r} 57 \\ -23 \\ \hline \end{array}
$$

$$
\begin{array}{r} 29 \\ -15 \\ \hline \end{array}
\qquad
\begin{array}{r} 74 \\ -51 \\ \hline \end{array}
\qquad
\begin{array}{r} 46 \\ -32 \\ \hline \end{array}
\qquad
\begin{array}{r} 69 \\ -35 \\ \hline \end{array}
\qquad
\begin{array}{r} 95 \\ -32 \\ \hline \end{array}
$$

Take It Away: 2 Digits

Directions: Study the steps for subtracting. Solve the problems using the steps.

Steps for Subtracting

1. Do you regroup? Yes, when the bottom number is bigger than the top.

2. Subtract the ones.

3. Subtract the tens.

tens	ones		tens	ones
3 ~~4~~	12	Regroup? Yes	3	7	Regroup? No
− 2	4		− 1	4
1	8		2	3

tens	ones
4	7
− 2	8

tens	ones
6	4
− 3	4

tens	ones
5	3
− 3	9

```
  56        83        43        75        91
 -27       -47       -39       -53       -18
```

```
  73        35        67        26        68
 -66       -14       -58       - 7       -45
```

Review

Directions: Add or subtract. Use regrouping when needed. Always do ones first and tens last.

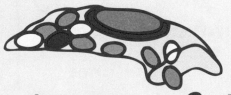

tens	ones		tens	ones		tens	ones
9	3		3	0		6	5
−2	5		+2	7		+1	7

7	6		8	2		5	6
−2	8		+1	9		−2	8

4	3		5	3		2	4
−1	4		−1	5		+5	7

```
  33            52            46
+47          +29          −37
```

Hundreds of Places

The place value of a digit or numeral is shown by where it is in the number. For example, in the number **123**, **1** has the place value of **hundreds**, **2** is **tens** and **3** is **ones**.

Directions: Study the examples. Then, write the missing numbers in the blanks.

Examples:

2 hundreds + 3 tens + 6 ones =

hundreds	tens	ones
2	3	6	= <u>236</u>

1 hundreds + 4 tens + 9 ones =

hundreds	tens	ones
1	4	9	= <u>149</u>

	hundreds	tens	ones	total
3 hundreds + 4 tens + 8 ones =	3	4	8	= _____
___ hundreds + ___ tens + ___ ones =	2	1	7	= _____
___ hundreds + ___ tens + ___ ones =	6	3	5	= _____
___ hundreds + ___ tens + ___ ones =	4	7	9	= _____
___ hundreds + ___ tens + ___ ones =	2	9	4	= _____
___ hundreds + 5 tens + 6 ones =	4	___	___	= _____
3 hundreds + 1 ten + 3 ones =	___	___	___	= _____
3 hundreds + ___ ten + 7 ones =	___	5	___	= _____
6 hundreds + 2 ten + ___ ones =	___		8	= _____

Add Attack: 3 Digits

Directions: Study the examples. Follow the steps to add.

Example:

Step 1:
Add the ones.

Step 2:
Add the tens.

Step 3:
Add the hundreds.

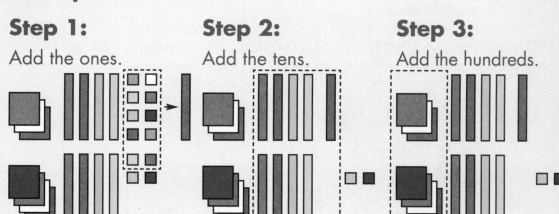

Do you regroup? Yes   Do you regroup? No

hundreds	tens	ones
	1	
3	4	8
+4	4	4
	2	

hundreds	tens	ones
	1	
3	4	8
+4	4	4
	9	2

hundreds	tens	ones
	1	
3	4	8
+4	4	4
7	9	2

hundreds	tens	ones
	1	
2	1	4
+2	3	8
4	5	2

hundreds	tens	ones
	1	
3	6	8
+2	1	3
___	8	1

hundreds	tens	ones
	1	
1	1	9
+5	6	5
___	___	4

$$418 \atop +323$$ $$471 \atop +319$$ $$334 \atop +528$$ $$659 \atop +127$$ $$736 \atop +145$$

Add Attack: 3 Digits

Directions: Study the example. Follow the steps to add. Regroup when needed.

Step 1: Add the ones.
Step 2: Add the tens.
Step 3: Add the hundreds.

hundreds	tens	ones
1	1	
3	4	8
+4	5	4
8	0	2

$10 = 1$ ten $+ 0$ ones

```
  348     172     575     623     369
 +214    +418    +329    +268    +533
```

```
  411     423     639     624     272
 +299    +169    +177    +368    +469
```

Take It Away: 3 Digits

Directions: Study the example. Follow the steps to subtract.

Step 1: Regroup ones.
Step 2: Subtract ones.
Step 3: Subtract tens.
Step 4: Subtract hundreds.

Example:

hundreds	tens	ones
	5	12
4	~~6~~	~~2~~
−2	5	3
2	0	9

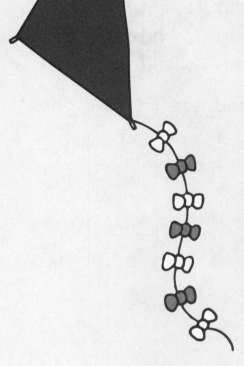

Directions: Draw a line to the correct answer. Color the kites.

347	144	963	762	287
−218	−135	−748	−553	−179

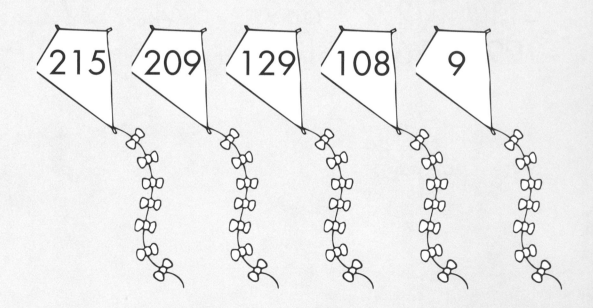

215 209 129 108 9

Take It Away: 3 Digits

Directions: Subtract. Circle the **7**'s that appear in the tens place.

score
257

$$\begin{array}{r} 492 \\ -221 \\ \hline 2\,7\,1 \end{array}$$

$$\begin{array}{r} 184 \\ -129 \\ \hline \end{array}$$

$$\begin{array}{r} 358 \\ -238 \\ \hline \end{array} \quad \begin{array}{r} 765 \\ -326 \\ \hline \end{array} \quad \begin{array}{r} 584 \\ -435 \\ \hline \end{array} \quad \begin{array}{r} 693 \\ -314 \\ \hline \end{array} \quad \begin{array}{r} 921 \\ -362 \\ \hline \end{array}$$

$$\begin{array}{r} 128 \\ -109 \\ \hline \end{array} \quad \begin{array}{r} 744 \\ -674 \\ \hline \end{array} \quad \begin{array}{r} 835 \\ -217 \\ \hline \end{array} \quad \begin{array}{r} 248 \\ -199 \\ \hline \end{array} \quad \begin{array}{r} 635 \\ -428 \\ \hline \end{array}$$

All in Place

Directions: Study the example. Write the missing numbers.

Example:

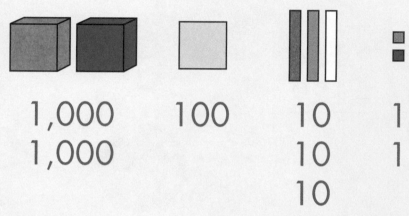

1,000   100   10   1
1,000   10   1
                  10

2 thousands + 1 hundred + **3** tens + 2 ones = **2,132**

5,286 = ___ thousands + ___ hundreds + ___ tens + ___ ones

1,831 = ___ thousands + ___ hundreds + ___ tens + ___ ones

8,972 = ___ thousands + ___ hundreds + ___ tens + ___ ones

4,528 = ___ thousands + ___ hundreds + ___ tens + ___ ones

3,177 = ___ thousands + ___ hundreds + ___ tens + ___ ones

Directions: Draw a line to the number that has:

8 hundreds	7,103
5 ones	2,862
9 tens	5,996
7 thousands	1,485

Fan-tastic!

Directions: Use the code to color the fan.

If the answer has:

9 thousands, color it **pink**.
6 thousands, color it **green**.
5 hundreds, color it **orange**.
8 tens, color it **red**.
3 ones, color it **blue**.

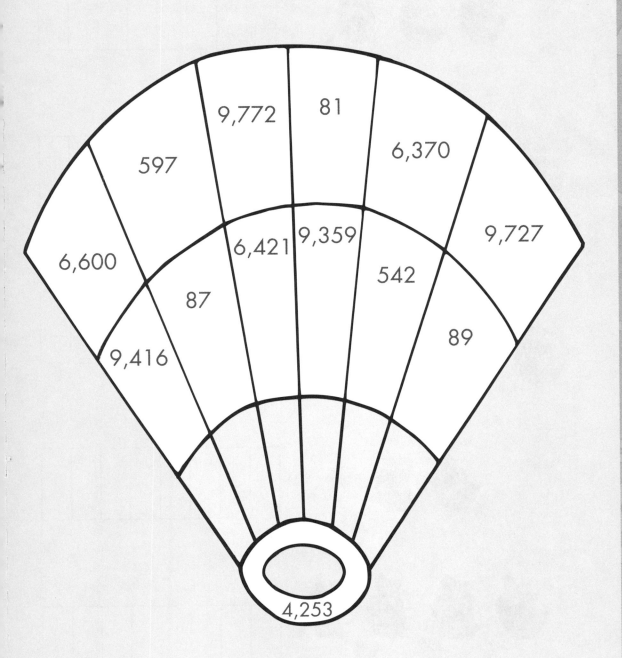

Take a Bite

A graph is a drawing that shows information about numbers.

Directions: Count the apples in each row. Color the boxes to show how many apples have bites taken out of them.

Example:

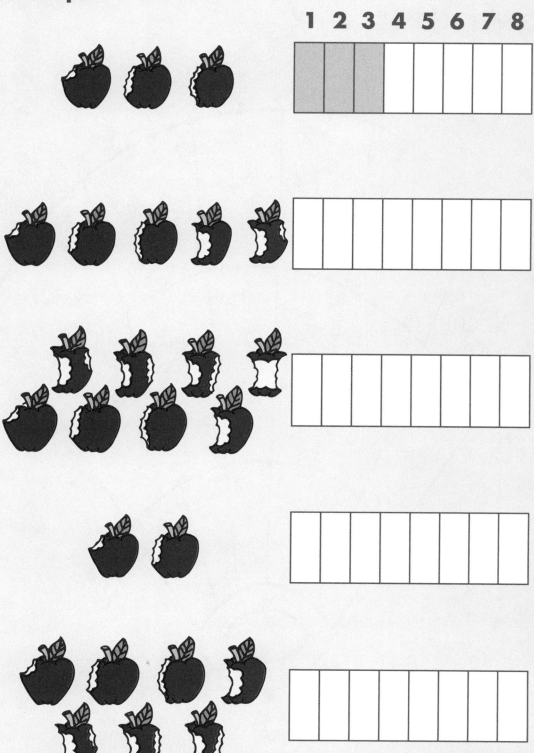

Something's Fishy!

Directions: Count the fish. Color the bowls to make a graph that shows the number of fish.

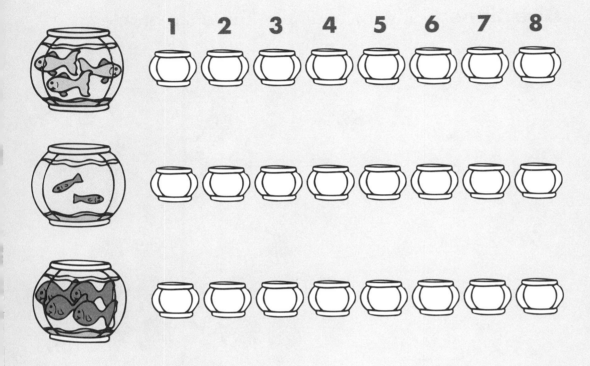

1 2 3 4 5 6 7 8

Directions: Use your fishbowl graphs to find the answers to the following questions. Draw a line to the correct bowl.

The most fish

The fewest fish

Bunches of Bugs

Multiplication is a short way to find the sum of adding the same number a certain amount of times. For example, **4 x 7 = 28** instead of **7 + 7 + 7 + 7 = 28**.

Directions: Study the example. Solve the problems.

Example:

3 + 3 + 3 = 9

3 threes = 9

3 x 3 = 9

7 + 7 = _____

2 sevens = _____

2 x 7 = _____

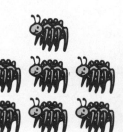

4 + 4 + 4 + 4 = _____

4 fours = _____

4 x _____ = _____

5 + 5 = _____

2 fives = _____

2 x _____ = _____

2 + 2 + 2 + 2 = _____

4 twos = _____

4 x _____ = _____

Good Times!

Directions: Study the example. Draw the groups and write the total.

Example:

3 x 2

2 + 2 + 2 = _____ 6 _____

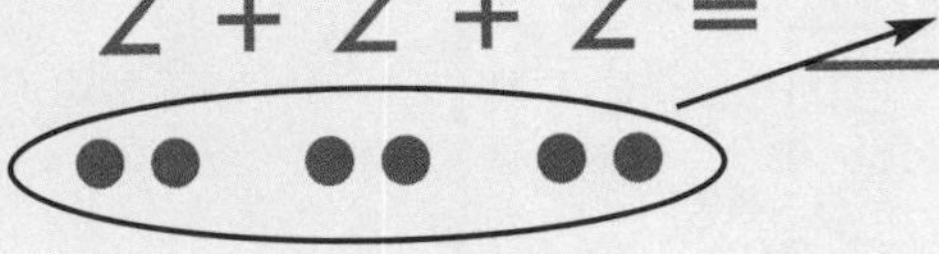

3 x 4

_____ + _____ + _____ = _____

2 x 5

_____ + _____ = _____

5 x 3

___ + ___ + ___ + ___ + ___ = _____

Focus on Fractions

A fraction is a number that names part of a whole, such as $\frac{1}{2}$ or $\frac{1}{3}$.

Directions: Study the examples. Color the correct fraction of each shape.

Examples:

shaded part   1
equal parts   2
$\frac{1}{2}$ (one-half) shaded

shaded part   1
equal parts   3
$\frac{1}{3}$ (one-third) shaded

shaded part   1
equal parts   4
$\frac{1}{4}$ (one-fourth) shaded

Color:

$\frac{1}{3}$ **red**

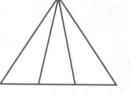 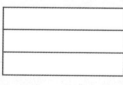 

Color:

$\frac{1}{4}$ **blue**

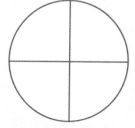  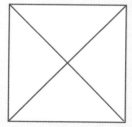

Color:

$\frac{1}{2}$ **orange**

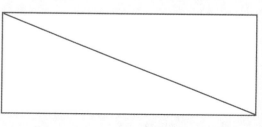 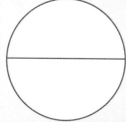

Made in the Shade

Directions: Study the examples. Circle the fraction that shows the shaded part. Then, circle the fraction that shows the white part.

Examples:

shaded   white

$\frac{1}{4}$ $\frac{1}{3}$ ⟨$\frac{1}{2}$⟩ $\frac{1}{3}$ ⟨$\frac{1}{2}$⟩ $\frac{1}{4}$

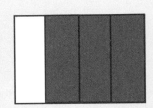

shaded   white

$\frac{1}{4}$ $\frac{1}{2}$ ⟨$\frac{3}{4}$⟩   ⟨$\frac{1}{4}$⟩ $\frac{2}{3}$ $\frac{1}{2}$

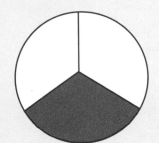

shaded   white

$\frac{1}{4}$ $\frac{1}{3}$ $\frac{1}{2}$ $\frac{2}{4}$ $\frac{2}{3}$ $\frac{2}{2}$

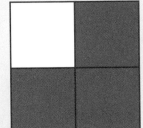

shaded   white

$\frac{3}{4}$ $\frac{1}{3}$ $\frac{3}{2}$ $\frac{1}{2}$ $\frac{1}{4}$ $\frac{1}{3}$

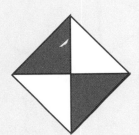

shaded   white

$\frac{2}{3}$ $\frac{2}{4}$ $\frac{2}{2}$ $\frac{1}{3}$ $\frac{2}{2}$ $\frac{2}{4}$

shaded   white

$\frac{2}{4}$ $\frac{2}{3}$ $\frac{2}{2}$ $\frac{1}{2}$ $\frac{1}{4}$ $\frac{1}{3}$

Get in Shape!

Geometry is mathematics that has to do with lines and shapes.

Directions: Color the shapes.

Color the triangles **blue**.

Color the circles **red**.

Color the squares green.

Color the rectangles **pink**.

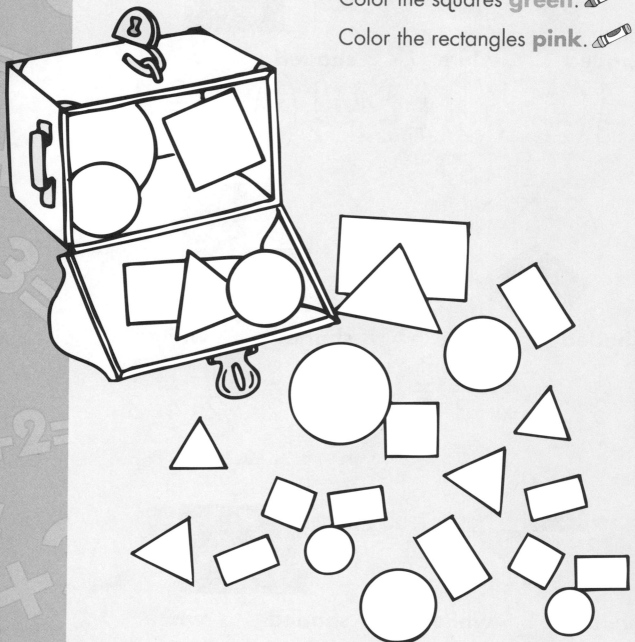

Tangram Tango

Directions: Cut out the tangram below. Mix up the pieces. Try to put it back together into a square.

This page is blank for the cutting activity
on the opposite side.

Measuring Up

Directions: Cut out the ruler. Measure each object to the nearest inch.

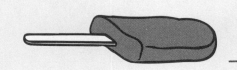

_____ inches

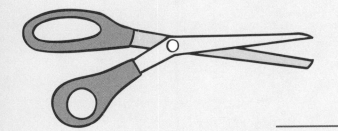

_____ inches

_____ inches

Directions: Measure objects around your house. Write the measurement to the nearest inch.

can of soup   _____ inches

pen   _____ inches

toothbrush   _____ inches

paper clip   _____ inches

small toy   _____ inches

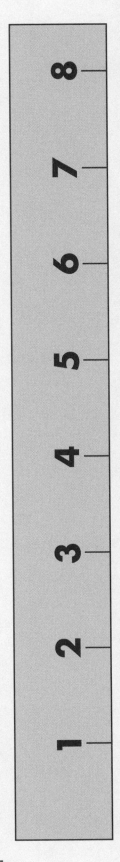

cut out

This page is blank for the cutting activity
on the opposite side.

Catch of the Day

Directions: Use the ruler to measure the fish to the nearest inch.

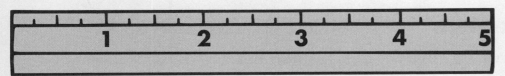

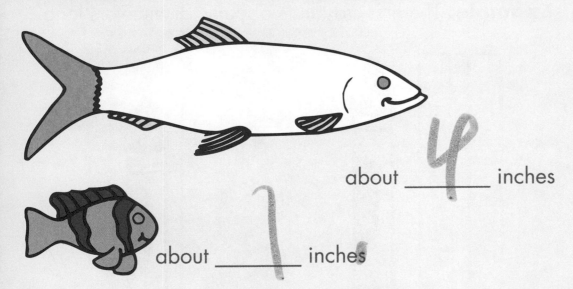

about __4__ inches

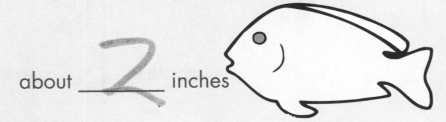

about __1__ inches

about __2__ inches

about __1__ inches

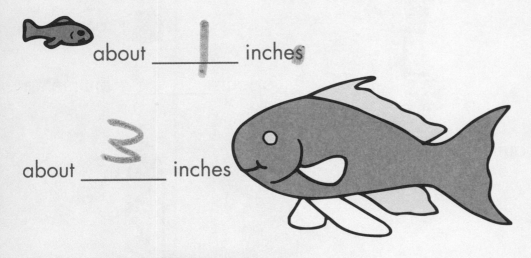

about __3__ inches

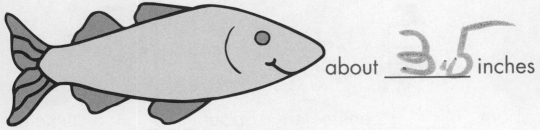

about __3.5__ inches

Centimeter Sense

A centimeter is a unit of length in the metric system. There are 2.54 centimeters in an inch.

Directions: Use a centimeter ruler to measure the crayons to the nearest centimeter.

Example: The first crayon is about 7 centimeters long.

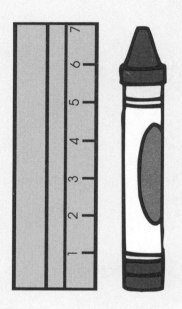

about ___7___ centimeters   about ___6___ centimeters

about _____ centimeters

about _____ centimeters

about _____ centimeters   about _____ centimeters

Hour by Hour

An hour is sixty minutes. The short hand of a clock tells the hour. It is written **0:00**, such as **5:00**. A half-hour is thirty minutes. When the long hand of the clock is pointing to the six, the time is on the half-hour. It is written **:30**, such as **5:30**.

Directions: Study the examples. Tell what time is on each clock.

Examples:

The minute hand is on the 12.
The hour hand is on the 9.
It is 9 o'clock.

9:00

The minute hand is on the 6.
The hour hand is *between* the 4 and 5.
It is 4:30.

4:30

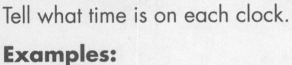

2:00   3:30   1:00   5:30

10:30   12:00   9:30   2:30

Time's Up!

The minute hand of a clock takes 5 minutes to move from one number to the next. Start at the 12 and count by fives to tell how many minutes it is past the hour.

Directions: Study the examples. Tell what time is on each clock.

Examples:

9:10   8:25

_____   _____   _____

_____   _____   _____

_____   _____   _____

Telling Time

Time can also be shown as fractions. 30 minutes = $\frac{1}{2}$ hour.

Directions: Shade the fraction of each clock and tell how many minutes you have shaded.

Example:

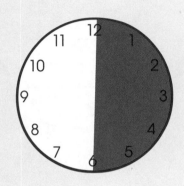

$\frac{1}{2}$ hour

30 minutes

$\frac{1}{4}$ hour

_____ minutes

$\frac{2}{4}$ hour

_____ minutes

$\frac{3}{4}$ hour

_____ minutes

$\frac{1}{2}$ hour

_____ minutes

Review

Counting

Directions: Write the number that is:

next   one less

68, 69, ____   ____, 57

786, 787, ____   ____, 650

one greater

12, ____

843, ____

Place Value: Tens & Ones

Directions: Draw a line to the correct number.

4 tens + 7 ones   20

2 tens + 0 ones   51

7 tens + 3 ones   47

5 tens + 1 one   73

Addition and Subtraction

Directions: Add or Subtract.

$$\begin{array}{ccccc} 15 & 14 & 7 & 8 & 10 \\ +\ 5 & -\ 4 & +\ 3 & -\ 6 & +7 \\ \hline \end{array}$$

Review

2-Digit Addition and Subtraction

Directions: Add or subtract using regrouping, if needed.

66 −37	38 +18	87 −69	52 −15	40 +17

84 +17	65 +14	99 −48	61 −36	56 +46

Place Value: Hundreds and Thousands

Directions: Draw a line to the correct number.

4 hundreds + 3 tens + 2 ones	7,201
6 hundreds + 7 tens + 6 ones	290
5 thousands + 3 hundreds + 7 tens + 2 ones	432
2 hundreds + 9 tens + 0 ones	676
7 thousands + 2 hundreds + 0 tens + 1 one	5,372

3-Digit Addition and Subtraction

Directions: Add or subtract, remembering to regroup, if needed.

458 −248	793 −414	822 −460	528 +319	697 +108

Review

Multiplication

Directions: Solve the problems. Draw groups if necessary.

2	6	3	8	5
x8	x4	x2	x4	x3

Fractions

Directions: Circle the correct fraction of each shape's white part.

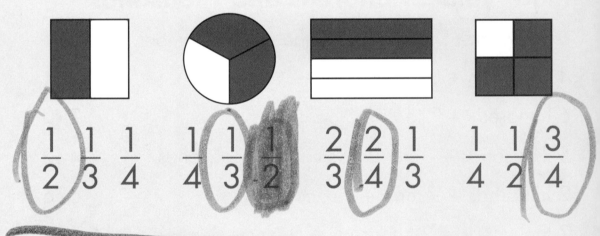

$$\frac{1}{2} \quad \frac{1}{3} \quad \frac{1}{4} \qquad \frac{1}{4} \quad \frac{1}{3} \quad \frac{1}{2} \qquad \frac{2}{3} \quad \frac{2}{4} \quad \frac{1}{3} \qquad \frac{1}{4} \quad \frac{1}{2} \quad \frac{3}{4}$$

Graphs

Directions: Count the flowers. Color the pots to make a graph that shows the number of flowers.

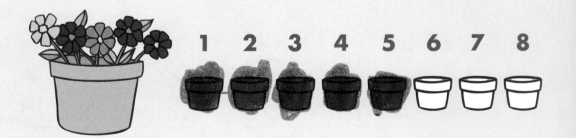

Review

Geometry

Directions: Match the shapes.

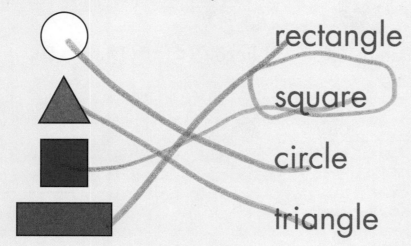

rectangle

square

circle

triangle

Measurement

Directions: Look at the ruler. Measure the objects to the nearest inch.

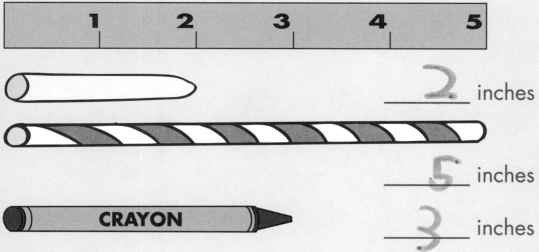

_2_ inches

_5_ inches

_3_ inches

Time

Directions: Tell what time is on each clock.

3:00   9:30   11:35   2:15

It All Makes Cents

Directions: Count the coins and write the amount.

Penny **1¢**　　　Nickel **5¢**　　　Dime **10¢**

_____ ¢

_____ ¢

_____ ¢

_____ ¢

_____ ¢

Time for a Change

Directions: Draw a line from the toy to the amount of money it costs.

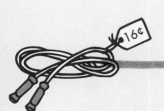

Counting Coins

A quarter is worth **25¢**.

Directions: Count the coins and write the amounts.

 _____ ¢

 _____ ¢

 _____ ¢

 _____ ¢

 _____ ¢

 _____ ¢

 _____ ¢

 _____ ¢

Get to the Point!

A decimal is a number with one or more places to the right of a decimal point, such as 6.5 or 2.25. Money amounts are written with two places to the right of the decimal point.

25¢   10¢   5¢   1¢

$.25 $.10 $.05 $.01

Directions: Count the coins and circle the amount shown.

Example:

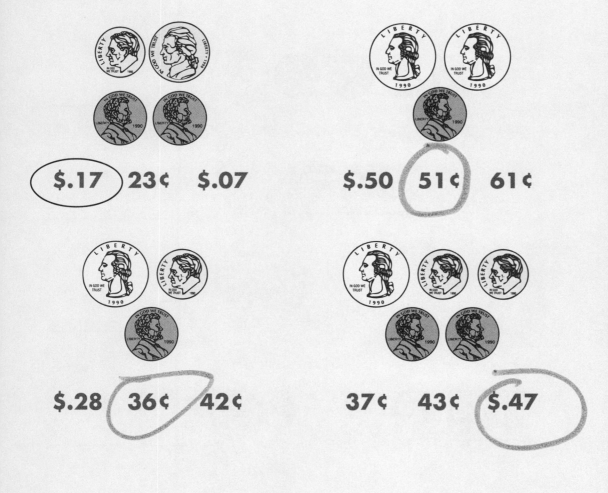

($.17)   23¢ $.07 $.50   (51¢)   61¢

$.28   (36¢)   42¢   37¢   43¢   ($.47)

Dollar Days

One dollar equals 100 cents. It is written $1.00.

Directions: Count the money and write the amounts.

 $____ . ____

 $____ . ____

 $____ . ____

 $____ . ____

 $____ . ____

 $____ . ____

 $____ . ____

 $____ . ____

Add It Up

Directions: Write the amount of money using decimals. Then, add to find the total amount.

Example:

$ <u>1</u> . <u>0 0</u>

 ___ . <u>0 5</u>

 + ___ . <u>0 2</u>

<u>1</u> . <u>0 7</u>

$ ___ . ____

$ ___ . ____

$ ___ . ____

+ $ ___ . ____

___ . ____

$ ___ . ____

$ ___ . ____

$ ___ . ____

+ $ ___ . ____

___ . ____

$ ___ . ____

$ ___ . ____

+ $ ___ . ____

___ . ____

$ ___ . ____

$ ___ . ____

$ ___ . ____

+ $ ___ . ____

___ . ____

A Day at the Park

Directions: Tell if you add, subtract or multiply. Then, write the answer.

Example:

There were 12 frogs sitting on a log by a pond, but 3 frogs hopped away. How many frogs are left?

_____Subtract_____ __9__ frogs

There are 9 flowers growing by the pond. Each flower has 2 leaves. How many leaves are there?

_____ _____ leaves

A tree had 7 squirrels playing in it. Then, 8 more came along. How many squirrels are there in all?

_____ _____ squirrels

There were 27 birds living in the trees around the pond, but 9 flew away. How many birds are left?

_____ _____ birds

Time to Solve It

Directions: Solve each problem.

Tracy wakes up at 7:00. She has
30 minutes before her bus comes.
What time does her bus come?

___ : _____

Vera walks her dog for 15 minutes
after supper. She finishes supper
at 6:30. When does she get home
from walking her dog?

___ : _____

Chip practices the piano for 30
minutes when he gets home from
school. He gets home at 3:30.
When does he stop practicing?

___ : _____

Tanya starts mowing the grass at
4:30. She finishes at 5:00. For
how many minutes does she mow
the lawn?

_____ minutes

Toy Time

Directions: Read each problem. Use the pictures to help you solve the problems.

Ben bought a ball. He had 11¢ left. How much money did he have at the start? _____ ¢

Tara has 75¢. She buys a car. How much money does she have left? _____ ¢

Leah wants to buy a doll and a ball. She has 80¢. How much more money does she need? _____ ¢

Jacob has 95¢. He buys the car and the ball. How much more money does he need to buy a doll for his sister? _____ ¢

Kim paid three quarters, one dime and three pennies for a hat. How much did it cost? _____ ¢

Addition: Putting together or adding two or more numbers to find the sum.

Adjectives: Words that tell more about a person, place or thing.

Alphabetical (ABC) Order: Putting letters or words in the order in which they appear in the alphabet.

Antonyms: Words that mean the opposite. Example: big and small.

Articles: Small words that help us to better understand nouns. Example: a and an.

Author: The person who wrote the words of a book.

Beginning Consonants: Consonant sounds that come at the beginning of words.

Blends: Two consonants put together to form a single sound.

Capital Letters: Letters that are used at the beginning of the names of people, places, days, months and holidays. Capital letters are also used at the beginning of sentences. These letters are sometimes called uppercase or "big" letters.

Centimeter: A measurement of length in the metric system. There are $2\frac{1}{2}$ centimeters in an inch.

Chapters: Small sections of a book.

Characters: The people or animals in a story.

Circle: A figure that is round.

Classifying: Putting things that are alike into groups.

Closed Figures: Figures whose lines connect.

Commands: Sentences that tell someone to do something.

Commutative Property: The rule in addition that states that, even if the order of the numbers is changed, the sum will be the same.

Compound Predicate: Predicate of the sentence formed by joining two verbs that have the same subject.

Compound Subject: Subject of the sentence formed by joining two nouns that have the same predicate.

Compound Words: Two words that are put together to make one new word. Example: house + boat = houseboat.

Comprehension: Understanding what you read.

Consonants: The letters b, c, d, f, g, h, j, k, l, m, n, p, q, r, s, t, v, w, x, y and z.

Consonant Blends: Two or three consonant letters in a word whose sounds combine, or blend. Examples: br, fr, gr, tr.

Consonant Teams: Two or three consonant letters that have the single sound. Examples: sh and tch.

Contractions: A short way to write two words together. Example: it is = it's.

Decimal: A number with one or more places to the right of a decimal point, such as 6.5 or 3.78. Money amounts are written with two places to the right of a decimal point, such as $1.30.

Dictionary: A reference book that gives the meaning of words and how to pronounce them.

Difference: The answer in a subtraction problem.

Digit: The symbols used to write numbers: 0, 1, 2, 3, 4, 5, 6, 7, 8 and 9.

Dime: Ten cents. It is written 10¢ or $.10.

Dollar: A dollar is equal to one hundred cents. It is written $1.00.

Double Vowel Words: When two vowels appear together in a word. Examples: tea, coat

Ending Consonants: Consonant sounds which come at the end of words.

Fact: Something that can be proven.

Fiction: A make-believe story.

Fraction: A number that names part of a whole, such as $\frac{1}{3}$ or $\frac{1}{2}$.

Geometry: Mathematics that has to do with lines and shapes.

Glossary: A little dictionary at the back of a book.

Graph: A drawing that shows information about numbers.

Guide Words: The words that appear at the top of a dictionary page to tell you what the first and the last words on that page will be.

Haiku: An Oriental form of poetry. Most have 5 syllables in the first and third lines, and 7 syllables in the middle line.

Half-Hour: Thirty minutes. It is written 0:30.

Hard and Soft c: In words where c is followed by a or u, the c usually has a hard sound (like a k). Examples: cup, cart. When c is followed by e, i or y, it usually has a soft sound (like an s). Examples: circle, fence.

Hard and Soft g: When g is followed by e, i or y, it usually has a soft sound (like j). Examples: change and gentle. The hard g sounds like the g in girl or gate.

Homophones: Words that sound the same but are spelled differently and mean different things. Example: blue and blew.

Hour: Sixty minutes. The short hand of a clock tells the hour. It is written 1:00.

Illustrator: The person who drew pictures for a book.

Inch: A unit of length in the standard measurement system.

Inference: A conclusion arrived at by what is suggested in the text.

Joining Words: Words that combine ideas in a sentence, such as "and," "but," "or" and "because."

Letter Teams: Two letters put together to make one new sound.

Long Vowels: Long vowels say their names. Examples: Long a is the sound you hear in hay. Long e is the sound you hear in me. Long i is the sound you hear in pie. Long o is the sound you hear in no. Long u is the sound you hear in cute.

Main Idea: The most important point or idea in a story.

Making Deductions: Using reasoning skills to draw conclusions.

Metric System: A system of measuring in which length is measured in millimeters, centimeters, meters and kilometers; capacity is measured in milliliters and liters; weight is measured in grams and kilograms; and temperature is measured in degrees Celsius.

Multiplication: A short way to find the sum of adding the same number a certain amount of times. For example, 7 x 4 = 28 instead of 7 + 7 + 7 + 7 = 28.

Nickel: Five cents. It is written 5¢ or $.05.

Nonfiction: A true story.

Nouns: Words that name a person, place or thing.

Open Figures: Figures whose lines do not connect.

Opinion: A feeling or belief about something that cannot be proven.

Opposites: Words that are different in every way. Example: black and white.

Ordinal Numbers: Numbers that indicate order in a series, such as first, second or third.

Pattern: Similar shapes or designs.

Penny: One cent. It is written 1¢ or $.01.

Place Value: The value of a digit, or numeral, shown by where it is in the number.

Plurals: Words that mean more than one. Examples: shoes, ladies, dishes, foxes.

Predicate: The verb in the sentence that tells the main action.

Predicting: Telling what is likely to happen, based on the facts.

Prefix: A syllable added at the beginning of a word to change its meaning. Examples: disappear, misplace.

Product: The answer of a multiplication problem.

Pronouns: Words that are used in place of nouns. "She," "he," "it" and "they" are pronouns.

Proper Nouns: The names of specific people, places and things. Proper nouns begin with a capital letter.

Quarter: Twenty-five cents. It is written 25¢ or $.25.

Questions: Sentences that ask something. A question begins with a capital letter and ends with a question mark.

R-Controlled Vowel: When r follows a vowel, it gives the vowel a different sound. Examples: her, bark, bird.

Rectangle: A figure with four corners and four sides. Sides opposite each other are the same length.

Regroup: To use ten ones to form one ten, ten tens to form 100, and so on.

Rhymes: Words that end with the same sound.

Rhyming Words: Words that sound alike at the end of a word. Example: cat and rat.

Same and Different: Being able to tell how things are the same and how they are different.

Sentences: A group of words that tells a complete idea or asks a question.

Sequencing: Putting things in the correct order, such as 7, 8, 9 or small, medium, large.

Short Vowels: Vowels that make short sounds. Examples: Short a is the sound you hear in cat. Short e is the sound you hear in leg. Short i is the sound you hear in pig. Short o is the sound in box. Short u is the sound in cup.

Silent Letters: Letters you can't hear at all, such as the gh in night, the w in wrong and the t in listen.

Simile: A figure of speech that compares two things that are alike in some way. The words "like" and "as" are used in similes. Examples: as soft as a pillow, as light as a feather.

Statements: Sentences that tell about something. Statements begin with a capital letter and end with a period.

Subtraction: Taking away or subtracting one number from another to find the difference.

Suffix: A syllable added at the end of a word to change its meaning. Examples: smaller, helpless.

Super Silent e: An e that you can't hear when it appears at the end of a word. It makes the other vowel have a long sound. Examples: cape, robe, slide.

Surprising Sentences: Sentences that tell a strong feeling. Surprising sentences begin with a capital letter and end with an exclamation point.

Syllables: The parts of words that have vowel sounds. Examples: Rab bit has two syllables. Bas ket ball has three syllables.

Synonyms: Words that mean the same or nearly the same. Example: sleepy and tired.

Table of Contents: A list at the beginning of a book, telling what is in the book and the page number.

Telling Sentences: Sentences that tell a strong feeling. Telling sentences begin with a capital letter and end with an exclamation point.

Title: The name of a book.

Tracking: Following a path.

Triangle: A figure with three corners and three sides.

Venn Diagram: A diagram that shows how two things are the same and how they are different.

Verbs: Words that tell the action in a sentence. Example: The boy ran fast.

Vowel Team: Vowels that appear together in words. Usually, the first one says its name and the second one is silent. Examples: leaf, soap, rain.

Vowels: The letters a, e, i, o, u and sometimes y.

Y as a Vowel: When y comes at the end of a word, it is a vowel. Examples: my, baby.

Alphabetical (ABC) order

Have your child alphabetize his/her word cards from the "Spelling Concentration" game.

Have your child list all the rainforest animals (or forest or ocean animals) that he/she can. Ask him/her to alphabetize the list on another sheet of paper. Give him/her extra help with words that begin with the same letter if needed.

Write the ABC's in a column down the left-hand side of a sheet of paper. As you read a story with your child, have him/her find and write words that begin with each letter.

Select a category. Then, help your child find a word for each letter of the alphabet that fits that category. Example: Animals—anteater, bear, cow, etc.

Help your child create tongue twisters using words in ABC order. Examples: A big cat danced elegantly. Frank gave Harry icky jellybeans.

Classifying

Have your child choose a topic and write a word list related to it. Example: Summer—hot, sun, bare feet, shorts, etc. He/she can create sentences using these words.

Help your child classify and list animals in groups: mammals, reptiles, fish, birds, amphibians, etc.

Creative Writing

Challenge your child to use his/her spelling words to create a "word find" for you to do.

Have your child make a list of rhyming words.

Have your child practice the spelling words by using all of them to create a story.

Have your child choose a topic, then write as many words as possible that fit the category. Example: volleyball: net, ball, uniform, serve, spike, bump, set, time out, sand, court, etc.

Expose your child to words with multiple meanings and have him/her look up the words in a dictionary. Have your child practice using the words in both written and spoken words.

Encourage your child to form similes with spelling words. A simile is a comparison using "like" or "as." Examples: He is as light as a feather. She is quiet like a mouse.

Help your child create a Family Book. Have your child add photos, draw pictures and write captions for an original family scrapbook.

Teach your child to write limericks. A limerick is a five-line humorous rhymed verse. Example: There once was a cat that was fat/ Who ate on a little red mat./ She said with a smile,/ "I've been here awhile,/ So you just go on now and scat!"

Create a story jar for your child. Write several tantalizing story starters on slips of paper. Some examples might be "If I found $100 . . ." or "What was that creaking sound I heard from the attic?" When your child needs a good idea for a story, he/she can draw a slip from the jar.

Dictionary Skills

Create a personal dictionary or a "Word Wall" poster for your child to keep track of each new word he/she learns.

Have a family "word of the week." Challenge family members to look up the word, to learn its spelling and to use it as much as possible during the week.

Make an alphabet book. Have your child cut big letters from magazines and glue each letter on a separate page. He/she can arrange the pages in ABC order. Then, have your child draw pictures of objects that start with each letter.

Choose a new word each day for your child to look up in the dictionary. Discuss the word's meaning. Have your child write a sentence using the new word. He/she can keep a list of the words in a word journal.

Help your child find new words on the Internet, in newspapers, on signs, etc. Have your child look them up in the dictionary. Make a collage using the words.

Following Directions

Have your child read and follow directions for constructing a model, playing a game, preparing a recipe, and so on. Ask your child to write his/her own directions for making a simple recipe or playing a simple game.

Geometry

Help your child cut out various geometric shapes and make a shape mobile to hang up.

Use construction paper to create prisms and three-dimensional objects, such as a party hat, a cube, etc.

Grammar

Have your child practice creating word families by adding "s" to the original word to make it mean more than one.

Write sentences for your child to proofread. Include both punctuation and spelling errors. Example: The bair went over the mountain?

Use your computer to write sentences for your child to correct. For example: The boys name is jim. Your child can gain valuable practice with both English skills and the computer by moving the arrow and delete keys to correct the sentence.

Graphs

Graph the birthdays of the people in your family. Ask your child questions based on the graph, such as "In which month are there the most birthdays?" "The fewest number?" "In which months are there no birthdays?"

Graph the people in your family, using criteria such as "boys," "girls," "pets," etc.

Inferences

Make riddle cards using clues for different fairy tale or cartoon characters. Play a guessing game with the cards. Let your child read the clues and name the character. Example: What little bear went hungry because a young girl ate his porridge? If you make these ahead of time, they can help pass the time on a long trip.

Put the pieces of a 12 to 20 piece puzzle in a bag. Let your child look at the pieces and make inferences about what the picture will be. Then, put the puzzle together.

Making Deductions

Put an object in a box and write clues for it. Have your child read the clues and guess what the object may be.

Measurement

Ask your child what other tools we use for measuring things (calendars and clocks to measure time, thermometer to measure temperature, etc.). Brainstorm a list of different measuring tools.

Show your child how to measure the circumference of cylindrical objects. For example, have your child predict the distance around a tree trunk. Pull a length of string around a tree trunk until the two ends meet. Cut the string. Then, measure the length of the string in inches and centimeters. Compare the actual measurement with your child's prediction.

Present a math word problem for your child to solve. Have him/her explain and write in sequence how to solve the problem.

Multiple-Meaning Words

Talk with your child about multiple-meaning words when opportunities present themselves in conversation. For example: "Did you hear the phone **ring**?" and "What a beautiful diamond **ring**!" Ask your child to brainstorm other examples of multiple-meaning words.

Parts of Speech

Play a fun "parts of speech" word game with your child. Write nouns, verbs and adjectives on index cards and have your child illustrate them. Then, let your child choose a noun card, a verb card and an adjective card and put them together to form fun sentences.

Have your child select a section of the newspaper and circle as many nouns and underline as many verbs as possible. You might ask him/her to circle plural nouns in a different color.

Patterns

Help your child find shape patterns as you drive or go for a walk together. Look for patterns in clothing, in billboards or on store signs.

Watch for word patterns as you read together. In the book *Too Much Noise* by Ann McGovern, your child can easily identify phrases that are repeated, and often, based on the story, predict the next phrase in the pattern.

Point of View

Read a chapter in a chapter book with your child. Then, ask your child to draw a picture of what happened in that chapter. You could also ask your child to draw a picture of what he/she thinks might happen next.

Read fairy tales like "The Three Little Pigs," "Cinderella," "The Three Billy Goats Gruff," "Hansel and Gretel," etc. Then, ask your child to retell the story from the point of view of the villain. Have him/her build a case explaining why the character did what he/she did.

Predicting Outcomes

While reading a story, stop periodically and have your child predict what he/she thinks will happen next.

Before reading a book with your child, ask him/her questions about the story and scan the illustrations. Ask questions beginning with who, what, why, when and how. For example: "What do you think this book is about?" "What do you think the title means?" "Who is this on the cover of the book?" "What is he/she doing?" "Do you think this is a true story or a make-believe story?"

Write an incomplete sentence using descriptive words but leave off the ending. Ask your child to finish the sentence. Example: The slinky, slimy lizard crept slowly into Marco's new, shiny bookbag and ___.

Recalling Details

Have your child choose a character from a story and write or tell about the character. Ask him/her to draw a picture of the character.

Read a fairy tale with your child. Ask him/her to tell or write the story from a different point of view. For example: Make the troll the good character in "Three Billy Goats Gruff" and the goats the bad characters.

Have your child make a story chart for a book, displaying the important events that happened at the beginning, middle and end of the story.

Your child can create a shoebox diorama displaying a scene from a favorite story, book, play, poem, and so on. A diorama is a three-dimensional scene that includes characters and objects from a story, displayed in an open box, similar to a stage. Encourage your child to be creative!

Relating to the Unknown

Choose a topic of interest to your child, such as insects, planets, sports, etc. Then, discuss what he/she knows and what he/she wants to learn about the topic. Formulate questions that will help your child learn new information based upon past knowledge. Example: How does a bee protect itself?

Retell

Read a book together. Then, ask your child to retell the story emphasizing what happened in the beginning, middle and end.

Rhymes

Make up silly sentences with your child to practice rhyming skills. For example, "I saw a paper star when I cleaned out the ___." You may also want to say a series of words and have your child tell you which one doesn't rhyme: coat, float, dish, goat.

Same and Different

Choose two animals, sports, toys, TV programs, etc. and ask your child to tell you how they are the same or how they are different.

Have your child compare three rooms in your home. Ask him/her to tell you how they are the same and how they are different.

Sentences

Create word or sentence "dot-to-dots." Instead of numbers, write letters or words. Have your child connect the dots in the correct sequence to write a word or to correctly order a sentence.

Play a game which helps your child learn to use words in context. Write several words on index cards. Take turns drawing a card and using the word on the card in a sentence.

Print sentences or copy a story on a sheet of paper. Leave blanks for key words. Have your child read the story and supply the missing words.

Write descriptive sentences on long cardboard strips. Have your child read the sentences. Then, cut the sentences into word sections and have your child put the sentences back in order.

Sequencing

Invite your child to recreate a story as a comic strip. List six or more important events or scenes from a story in sequence. Then, have your child write each event on a separate sheet of paper and draw an accompanying picture. Glue the pages in order on large sheets of colorful construction paper.

Write or tell a story together. Begin the story. After a few sentences, have your child continue the story. Take turns until you get to the end.

Use the comics to help your child practice sequence. Select comics that show a simple sequence, and read the comic strip with your child. Cut the comic strip apart, and challenge your child to rearrange it in the correct order. You could also draw simple pictures in a series, and have your child draw a picture to show what would happen next. Pictures from the family photo album are also fun to sequence. Your child can use the visual clues of growth to help arrange them in sequential order.

Spelling

Create a deck of cards with letters and letter teams. Have your child try to make words from the cards drawn.

Write each of your child's spelling words on an index card. Cut apart the cards at the syllables. Mix up the cards and have your child try to put the original words back together.

Play "Spell-o" with your child. Write each word in a box on a 5 x 5 grid. As you name a spelling word, have your child spell it back to you. He/she can then cover the square. When the card has five in a row covered, your child has "Spell-o!"

Fill a squirt bottle with water and let your child spell words by squirting water on dry pavement.

Challenge your child to think of as many words as possible with letter teams such as oy. Try other letter teams such as au, aw, ee and ow. Allow your child to check a dictionary if he/she needs to.

Synonyms, Antonyms, Homophones

Encourage your child to create more varied and interesting sentences by substituting synonyms for words he/she uses repeatedly. As your child reads his/her writing to you, point out places where a synonym might be used, such as the use of the words "tiny" or "small" instead of "little."

Teach your child how to use a thesaurus to find synonyms (words that have almost the same meaning) of each spelling word. A thesaurus organized like a dictionary is the easiest to use.

Make a synonym memory game with your child. Write ten words on index cards. Then, write synonyms for the words on additional index cards. Mix up the cards and place them facedown to play. Let your child turn over two cards at a time. If he/she matches two words which are synonyms, he/she gets to keep the cards. If the two words do not match, he/she must return the cards to their position. Then, the next player takes his/her turn. Play continues until all of the cards are gone. This game may also be played with words and their antonyms.

Act out a word (hello) from your list of antonyms and ask your child to act out the antonym (goodbye).

Create a list of antonyms or homophones with your child. Then, ask your child to write a poem or limerick using the words.

Using the list of homophones, ask your child to write and illustrate sentences using a pair of homophones. Examples: I have a pair of pears. The bear had bare feet.

Time

Help your child create a paper plate clock. Use a paper fastener to attach the minute and hour hands. Suggest different hour and half-hour times for your child to show on the clock face.

Tracking

Draw a map of your home or neighborhood. Have your child draw paths from your home to other places in the area. Go for a walk or a drive, following one of the paths your child drew.

Have your child write, in order, how to escape from your home in case of an emergency. Then, follow the path with your family.

Visualizing

Ask your child to form a picture of a memory in his/her mind. Then, ask him/her to write or draw a description of what he/she sees.

Cut out pictures of scenery from old magazines. Share the pictures with your child. Ask him/her to tell you what images come to mind as he/she views them.

224

ANSWER KEY

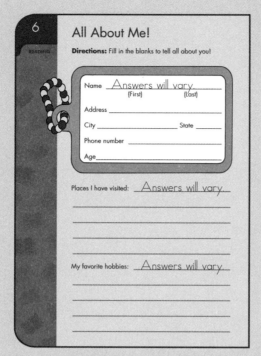

6

All About Me!

Directions: Fill in the blanks to tell all about you!

Name _Answers will vary._
(First)   (Last)

Address _____

City _____ State _____

Phone number _____

Age _____

Places I have visited: _Answers will vary._
_____
_____
_____

My favorite hobbies: _Answers will vary._
_____
_____
_____

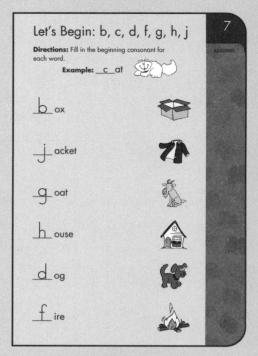

7

Let's Begin: b, c, d, f, g, h, j

Directions: Fill in the beginning consonant for each word.

Example: _c_ at

_b_ ox

_j_ acket

_g_ oat

_h_ ouse

_d_ og

_f_ ire

8

Let's Begin: k, l, m, n, p, q, r

Directions: Write the letter that makes the beginning sound for each picture.

_m_   _q_   _r_

_n_   _m_   _l_

_k_   _r_   _q_

_p_   _n_   _m_

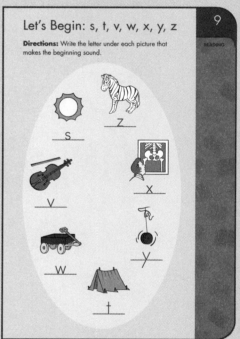

9

Let's Begin: s, t, v, w, x, y, z

Directions: Write the letter under each picture that makes the beginning sound.

_s_   _z_

_v_   _x_

_w_   _y_

_t_

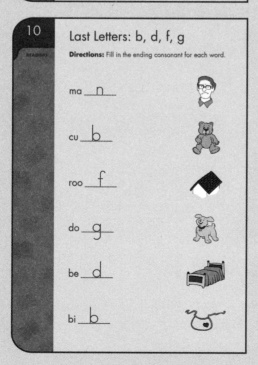

10

Last Letters: b, d, f, g

Directions: Fill in the ending consonant for each word.

ma _n_

cu _b_

roo _f_

do _g_

be _d_

bi _b_

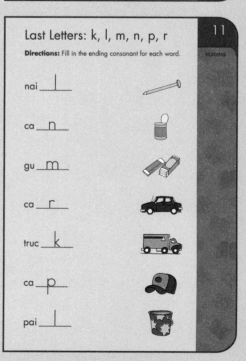

11

Last Letters: k, l, m, n, p, r

Directions: Fill in the ending consonant for each word.

nai _l_

ca _n_

gu _m_

ca _r_

truc _k_

ca _p_

pai _l_

12 — Last Letters: s, t, x

Directions: Fill in the ending consonant for each word.

ca **t**

bo **x**

bu **s**

fo **x**

boa **t**

ma **t**

13 — Bring on the Blends!

Consonant blends are two or three consonant letters in a word whose sounds combine, or blend. **Examples: br, fr, gr, pr, tr**

Directions: Look at each picture. Say its name. Write the blend you hear at the beginning of each word.

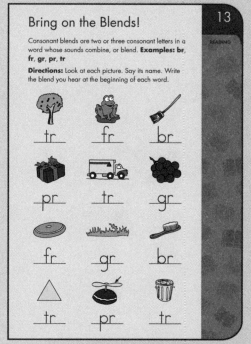

tr   fr   br

pr   tr   gr

fr   gr   br

tr   pr   tr

14 — Blends: fl, br, pl, sk, sn

Blends are two consonants put together to form a single sound.

Directions: Look at the pictures and say their names. Write the letters for the beginning sound in each word.

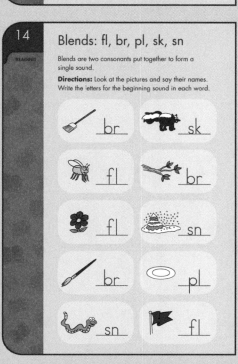

br   sk

fl   br

fl   sn

br   pl

sn   fl

15 — Blends: bl, sl, cr, cl

Directions: Look at the pictures and say their names. Write the letters for the beginning sound in each word.

cl own   bl anket   cr ayon

cl ock   sl ide   cl oud

sl ed   cr ab   cr ocodile

16 — Tell Me a Riddle

Directions: Write a word from the word box to answer each riddle.

| clock | blow | climb | slipper |
| gloves | clap | blocks | flashlight |

1. You need me when the lights go out.
   What am I? flashlight
2. People use me to tell the time.
   What am I? clock
3. You put me on your hands in the winter to keep them warm.
   What am I? gloves
4. Cinderella lost one like me at midnight.
   What am I? slipper
5. This is what you do with your hands when you are pleased.
   What is it? clap
6. You can do this with a whistle or with bubble gum.
   What is it? blow
7. These are what you might use to build a castle when you are playing.
   What are they? blocks
8. You do this to get to the top of a hill.
   What is it? climb

17 — Teammates

Consonant teams are two or three consonant letters that have a single sound. **Examples: sh and tch**

Directions: Write each word from the word box next to its picture. Underline the consonant team in each word. Circle the consonant team in each word in the box.

| bench | match | shoe | thimble | shell |
| peach | watch | whale | chair | wheel |

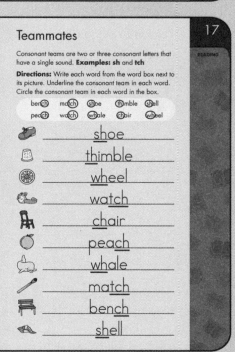

shoe
thimble
wheel
watch
chair
peach
whale
match
bench
shell

18 Join the Team

Directions: Look at the first picture in each row. Circle the pictures that have the same sound.

19 Sort It Out

Directions: Look at the words in the word box. Write all of the words that end with the **ng** sound in the column under the picture of the **ring**. Write all of the words that end with the **nk** sound under the picture of the **sink**. Finish the sentences with words from the word box.

strong rank bring bank honk hang thank
long hunk song stung bunk sang junk

ng	nk
strong	rank
long	hunk
bring	bank
song	honk
stung	bunk
hang	thank
sang	junk

1. _Honk_ your horn when you get to my house.
2. He was _stung_ by a bumblebee.
3. We are going to put our money in a _bank_.
4. I want to _thank_ you for the birthday present.
5. My brother and I sleep in _bunk_ beds.

20 Shhh! Silent Letters

Some words have letters you can't hear at all, such as the **gh** in **night**, the **w** in **wrong**, the **l** in **walk**, the **k** in **knee**, the **b** in **climb** and the **t** in **listen**.

Directions: Look at the words in the word box. Write the word under its picture. Underline the silent letters.

knife light calf wrench lamb eight
wrist whistle comb thumb knob knee

eig<u>h</u>t   <u>wr</u>ist   <u>kn</u>ee

cal<u>f</u>   lam<u>b</u>   <u>kn</u>ob

<u>wh</u>istle   lig<u>h</u>t   <u>wr</u>ench

com<u>b</u>   t<u>h</u>umb   <u>kn</u>ife

21 Review

Directions: Read the story. Circle the consonant teams (two or three letters) and silent letters in the underlined words. Be sure to check for more than one team in a word! One has been done for you.

One day last Spring my family went on a picnic. My father picked out a pretty spot next to a stream. While my brother and I climbed a tree, my mother spread out a sheet and placed the food on it. But before we could eat, a skunk walked out of the woods! Mother screamed and scared the skunk. It sprayed us with a terrible smell! Now, we think it is a funny story. But that day, we ran!

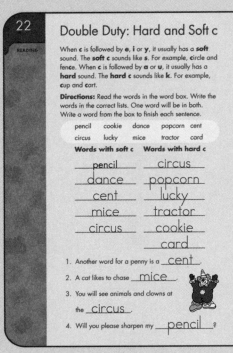

Directions: Write the words with three-letter blends on the lines.

Spring
stream
spread
screamed
sprayed

22 Double Duty: Hard and Soft c

When **c** is followed by **e**, **i** or **y**, it usually has a **soft** sound. The **soft c** sounds like **s**. For example, **c**ircle and fen**c**e. When **c** is followed by **a** or **u**, it usually has a **hard** sound. The **hard c** sounds like **k**. For example, **c**up and **c**art.

Directions: Read the words in the word box. Write the words in the correct lists. One word will be in both. Write a word from the box to finish each sentence.

pencil cookie dance popcorn cent
circus lucky mice tractor card

Words with soft c	**Words with hard c**
pencil	circus
dance	popcorn
cent	lucky
mice	tractor
circus	cookie
	card

1. Another word for a penny is a _cent_.
2. A cat likes to chase _mice_.
3. You will see animals and clowns at the _circus_.
4. Will you please sharpen my _pencil_?

23 Double Duty: Hard and Soft g

When **g** is followed by **e**, **i** or **y**, it usually has a **soft** sound. The **soft g** sounds like **j**. **Example:** chan**g**e and **g**entle. The **hard g** sounds like the **g** in **g**irl or **g**ate.

Directions: Read the words in the word box. Write the words in the correct lists. Write a word from the box to finish each sentence.

engine glove cage
magic frog giant
flag large glass
goose

Words with soft g	**Words with hard g**
engine	glove
giant	flag
cage	glass
large	frog
magic	goose

1. Our bird lives in a _cage_.
2. Pulling a rabbit from a hat is a good _magic_ trick.
3. A car needs an _engine_ to run.
4. A _giant_ is a huge person.
5. An elephant is a very _large_ animal.

24 — Letter Detector: Short Vowels

Vowels can make **short** or **long** sounds. The **short a** sounds like the **a** in c**a**t. The **short e** is like the **e** in l**e**g. The **short i** sounds like the **i** in p**i**g. The **short o** sounds like the **o** in b**o**x. The **short u** sounds like the **u** in c**u**p.

Directions: Look at each picture. Write the missing short vowel letter.

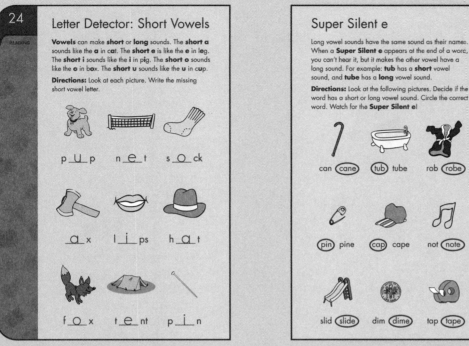

p u p   n e t   s o ck

a x   l i ps   h a t

f o x   t e nt   p i n

25 — Super Silent e

Long vowel sounds have the same sound as their names. When a **Super Silent e** appears at the end of a word, you can't hear it, but it makes the other vowel have a long sound. For example: **tub** has a **short** vowel sound, and **tube** has a **long** vowel sound.

Directions: Look at the following pictures. Decide if the word has a short or long vowel sound. Circle the correct word. Watch for the **Super Silent e**!

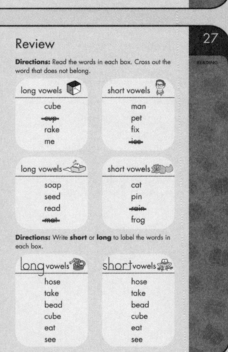

can (cane)   (tub) tube   rob (robe)

(pin) pine   (cap) cape   not (note)

slid (slide)   dim (dime)   tap (tape)

26 — Letter Detector: Long Vowels

Directions: Say the name of the pictures. Listen for the long vowel sounds. Write the missing long vowel sound under each picture.

c a ke   h i ke   n o se

a pe   c u be   gr a pe

r a ke   b o ne   k i te

27 — Review

Directions: Read the words in each box. Cross out the word that does not belong.

long vowels	short vowels
cube	man
~~cup~~	pet
rake	fix
me	~~ice~~

long vowels	short vowels
soap	cat
seed	pin
read	~~rain~~
~~mat~~	frog

Directions: Write **short** or **long** to label the words in each box.

long vowels	short vowels
hose	hose
take	take
bead	bead
cube	cube
eat	eat
see	see

28 — R in Charge

When a vowel is followed by the letter **r**, it has a different sound.

Example: he and **her**

Directions: Write a word from the word box to finish each sentence. Notice the sound of the vowel followed by an **r**.

park	chair	horse	bark	bird
hurt	girl	hair	store	ears

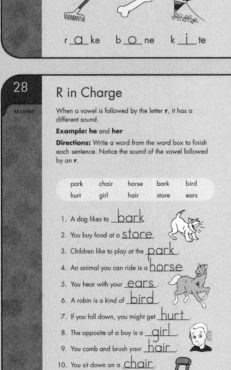

1. A dog likes to _bark_
2. You buy food at a _store_
3. Children like to play at the _park_
4. An animal you can ride is a _horse_
5. You hear with your _ears_
6. A robin is a kind of _bird_
7. If you fall down, you might get _hurt_
8. The opposite of a boy is a _girl_
9. You comb and brush your _hair_
10. You sit down on a _chair_

29 — Double Trouble

Usually when two vowels appear together, the first one says its name and the second one is silent.

Example: bean

Directions: Unscramble the double vowel words below. Write the correct word on the line.

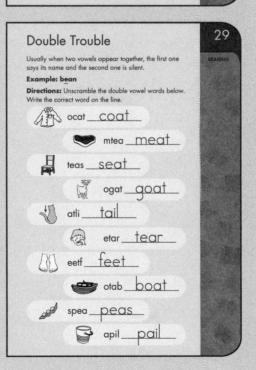

ocat _coat_

mtea _meat_

teas _seat_

ogat _goat_

atli _tail_

etar _tear_

eetf _feet_

otab _boat_

spea _peas_

apil _pail_

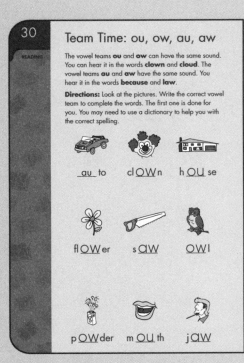

30 READING

Team Time: ou, ow, au, aw

The vowel teams **ou** and **ow** can have the same sound. You can hear it in the words **clown** and **cloud**. The vowel teams **au** and **aw** have the same sound. You hear it in the words **because** and **law**.

Directions: Look at the pictures. Write the correct vowel team to complete the words. The first one is done for you. You may need to use a dictionary to help you with the correct spelling.

_au_ to   cl_OW_n   h_OU_se

fl_OW_er   s_aw_   _OW_l

p_OW_der   m_OU_th   j_aw_

31 READING

Team Time: ea

The vowel team **ea** can have a **short e** sound like in **head**, or a **long e** sound like in **bead**. An **ea** followed by an **r** makes a sound like the one in **ear** or like the one in **heard**.

Directions: Read the story. Listen for the sound **ea** makes in the bold words.

Have you ever **read** a book or **heard** a story about a **bear**? You might have **learned** that bears sleep through the winter. Some bears may sleep the whole **season**. Sometimes they look almost **dead**! But they are very much alive. As the cold winter passes and the spring **weather** comes **near**, they wake up. After such a nice rest, they must be **ready** to **eat** a **really** big **meal**!

words with long ea

season
eat
really
meal

words with short ea   **ea followed by r**

read   heard
dead   bear
weather   learned
ready   near

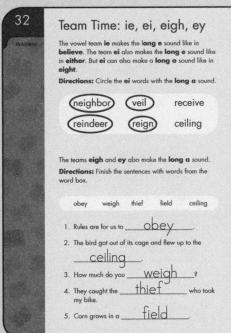

32 READING

Team Time: ie, ei, eigh, ey

The vowel team **ie** makes the long e sound like in **believe**. The team **ei** also makes the **long e** sound like in **either**. But **ei** can also make a **long a** sound like in **eight**.

Directions: Circle the **ei** words with the **long a** sound.

(neighbor)   (veil)   receive

(reindeer)   (reign)   ceiling

The teams **eigh** and **ey** also make the **long a** sound.

Directions: Finish the sentences with words from the word box.

| obey | weigh | thief | field | ceiling |

1. Rules are for us to _obey_.
2. The bird got out of its cage and flew up to the _ceiling_.
3. How much do you _weigh_?
4. They caught the _thief_ who took my bike.
5. Corn grows in a _field_.

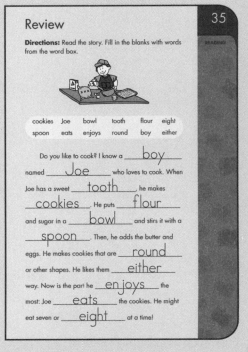

33 READING

Team Time: oi, oy, ou, ow

Directions: Look at the first picture in each row. Circle the pictures that have the same sound.

oil

toy

couch

howl

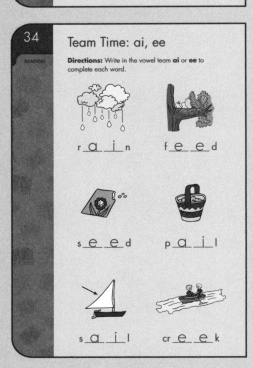

34 READING

Team Time: ai, ee

Directions: Write in the vowel team **ai** or **ee** to complete each word.

r_ai_n   f_ee_d

s_ee_d   p_ai_l

s_ai_l   cr_ee_k

35 READING

Review

Directions: Read the story. Fill in the blanks with words from the word box.

| cookies | Joe | bowl | tooth | flour | eight |
| spoon | eats | enjoys | round | boy | either |

Do you like to cook? I know a _boy_ named _Joe_ who loves to cook. When Joe has a sweet _tooth_, he makes _cookies_. He puts _flour_ and sugar in a _bowl_ and stirs it with a _spoon_. Then, he adds the butter and eggs. He makes cookies that are _round_ or other shapes. He likes them _either_ way. Now is the part he _enjoys_ the most: Joe _eats_ the cookies. He might eat seven or _eight_ at a time!

36 That's Y!

When **y** comes at the end of a word, it is a vowel. When **y** is the only vowel at the end of a one-syllable word, it has the sound of a **long i** (like in **my**). When **y** is the only vowel at the end of a word with more than one syllable, it has the sound of a **long e** (like in **baby**).

Directions: Look at the words in the word box. If the word has the sound of a **long i**, write it under the word **my**. If the word has the sound of a **long e**, write it under the word **baby**. Write the word from the word box that answers each riddle.

| happy | penny | fry | try | dry |
| bunny | windy | sky | party | fly |

my	**baby**
fry	happy
try	bunny
sky	penny
dry	windy
fly	party

1. It takes five of these to make a nickel. penny
2. This is what you call a baby rabbit. bunny
3. It is often blue and you can see it if you look up. sky
4. You might have one of these on your birthday. party

37 Putting It Together

Compound words are two words that are put together to make one new word.

Directions: Read the sentences. Fill in the blank with a compound word from the box.

| raincoat bedroom lunchbox hallway sandbox |

1. A box with sand is a sandbox
2. The way through a hall is a hallway
3. A box for lunch is a lunchbox
4. A coat for the rain is a raincoat
5. A room with a bed is a bedroom

38 What's Cooking?

Compound words are formed by putting together two smaller words.

Directions: Help the cook brew her stew. Mix words from the first column with words from the second column to make new words. Write your new words on the lines at the bottom.

grand	brows
snow	light
eye	stairs
down	string
rose	book
shoe	mother
note	ball
moon	bud

1. grandmother
2. snowball
3. eyebrows
4. downstairs
5. rosebud
6. shoestring
7. notebook
8. moonlight

39 Two-for-One Special

Directions: Draw a line under the compound word in each sentence. On the line, write the two words that make up the compound word.

1. A firetruck came to help put out the fire. fire truck
2. I will be nine years old on my next birthday. birth day
3. We built a treehouse at the back. tree house
4. Dad put a scarecrow in his garden. scare crow
5. It is fun to make footprints in the snow. foot prints
6. I like to read the comics in the newspaper. news paper
7. Cowboys ride horses and use lassos. cow boys

40 Short and Sweet

Contractions are a short way to write two words, such as **isn't, I've** and **weren't. Example: it is = it's**

Directions: Draw a line from each word pair to its contraction.

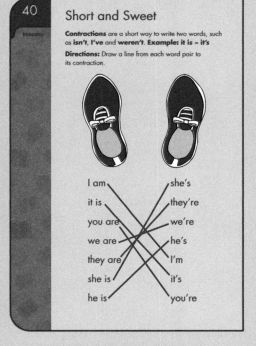

I am	she's
it is	they're
you are	we're
we are	he's
they are	I'm
she is	it's
he is	you're

41 We Love Contractions!

Directions: Cut out the two words and put them together to show what two words make the contraction. Glue them over the contraction.

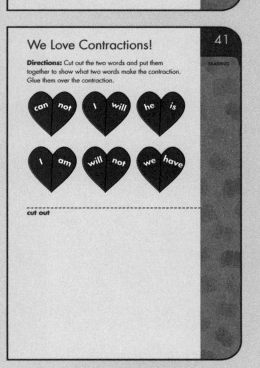

| can | not | I | will | he | is |
| I | am | will | not | we | have |

- - - - - - - - - - - - - - - - - - - -
cut out

Put Your Hands Together

43 · READING

Words are made up of parts called **syllables**. Each syllable has a vowel sound. One way to count syllables is to clap as you say the word.

Example:

cat	1 clap	1 syllable
table	2 claps	2 syllables
butterfly	3 claps	3 syllables

Directions: "Clap out" the words below. Write how many syllables each word has.

movie	2
piano	3
tree	1
bicycle	3
sun	1
cabinet	3
football	2
dog	1
basket	2
swimmer	2
rainbow	2
paper	2
picture	2

Give Me a Break

44 · READING

Dividing a word into syllables can help you read a new word. You also might divide syllables when you are writing if you run out of space on a line. Many words contain two consonants that are next to each other. A word can usually be divided between two consonants.

Directions: Divide each word into two syllables. The first one is done for you.

kitten	kit	ten
lumber	lum	ber
batter	bat	ter
winter	win	ter
funny	fun	ny
harder	hard	er
dirty	dir	ty
sister	sis	ter

Break it Up!

45 · READING

When a double consonant is used in the middle of a word, the word can usually be divided between the consonants.

Directions: Look at the words in the word box. Divide each word into two syllables. Leave space between each syllable. One is done for you.

butter	puppy	kitten	yellow
dinner	chatter	ladder	happy
pillow	letter	mitten	summer

but ter	chat ter	mit ten
din ner	let ter	yel low
pil low	kit ten	hap py
pup py	lad der	sum mer

Many words are divided between two consonants that are not alike.

Directions: Look at the words in the word box. Divide each word into two syllables. One is done for you.

window	doctor	number
mister	winter	pencil
barber	sister	picture

win dow	doc tor	num ber
mis ter	win ter	pen cil
bar ber	sis ter	pic ture

Add It On

46 · READING

A **suffix** is a syllable that is added at the end of a word to change its meaning.

Directions: Add the suffixes to the root words to make new words. Use your new words to complete the sentences.

help + ful = helpful
care + less = careless
talk + ed = talked
love + ly = lovely
loud + er = louder

1. My mother talked to my teacher about my homework.
2. The radio was louder than the television.
3. Sally is always helpful to her mother.
4. The flowers are lovely.
5. It is careless to cross the street without looking both ways.

Backward Nan

47 · READING

Directions: Read the story. Underline the words that end with **est**, **ed** or **ing**. On the lines below, write the root words for each word you underlined.

The funniest book I ever read was about a girl named Nan. Nan did everything backward. She even spelled her name backward. Nan slept in the day and played at night. She dried her hair before washing it. She turned on the light after she finished her book—which she read from the back to the front! When it rained, Nan waited until she was inside before opening her umbrella. She even walked backward. The silliest part: The only thing Nan did forward was back up!

1. funny	8. finish
2. name	9. rain
3. spell	10. wait
4. play	11. open
5. dry	12. walk
6. wash	13. silly
7. turn	

The Three Rs

48 · READING

Prefixes are syllables added to the beginning of words that change their meaning. The prefix **re** means "again."

Directions: Read the story. Then, follow the instructions.

Kim wants to find ways she can save the Earth. She studies the "three R's"—reduce, reuse and recycle. Reduce means to make less. Both reuse and recycle mean to use again.

Add **re** to the beginning of each word below. Use the new words to complete the sentences.

re build	re fill
re read	re tell
re write	re run

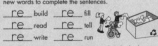

1. The race was a tie, so Dawn and Kathy had to rerun it.
2. The block wall fell down, so Simon had to rebuild it.
3. The water bottle was empty, so Luna had to refill it.
4. Javier wrote a good story, but he wanted to rewrite it to make it better.
5. The teacher told a story, and students had to retell it.
6. Toni didn't understand the directions, so she had to reread them.

Prefix Power — 49

Directions: Change the meaning of the sentences by adding the prefixes to the **bold** words.

The boy was **lucky** because he guessed the answer **correctly**.

The boy was (un) __unlucky__ because he guessed the answer (in) __incorrectly__.

When Mary **behaved**, she felt **happy**.

When Mary (mis) __misbehaved__, she felt (un) __unhappy__.

Mike wore his jacket **buttoned** because the dance was **formal**.

Mike wore his jacket (un) __unbuttoned__ because the dance was (in) __informal__.

Tim **understood** because he was **familiar** with the book.

Tim (mis) __misunderstood__ because he was (un) __unfamiliar__ with the book.

Review — 50

Directions: Read each sentence. Look at the words in **bold**. Circle the prefix and write the root word on the line.

1. The (pre)**view** of the movie was funny. __view__
2. We always drink (non)**fat** milk. __fat__
3. We will have to (re)**schedule** the trip. __schedule__
4. Are you tired of (re)**runs** on television? __run__
5. I have (out)**grown** my new shoes already. __grow__
6. You must have (mis)**placed** the papers. __place__
7. Police (en)**force** the laws of the city. __force__
8. I (dis)**liked** that book. __like__
9. The boy (dis)**trusted** the big dog. __trust__
10. Try to (en)**joy** yourself at the party. __joy__

Mike's Bike — 51

Directions: Read the story about bike safety. Answer the questions below the story.

Mike has a red bike. He likes his bike. Mike wears a helmet. Mike wears knee pads and elbow pads. They keep him safe. Mike stops at signs. Mike looks both ways. Mike is safe on his bike.

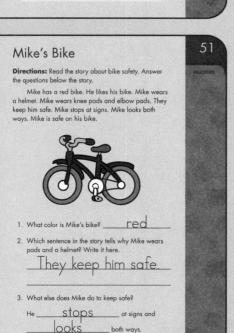

1. What color is Mike's bike? __red__
2. Which sentence in the story tells why Mike wears pads and a helmet? Write it here.
   __They keep him safe.__
3. What else does Mike do to keep safe?
   He __stops__ at signs and __looks__ both ways.

Total Recall — 52

Directions: Read about Nikki's pets. Then, answer the questions.

Nikki has two cats, Tiger and Sniffer, and two dogs, Spot and Wiggles. Tiger is an orange striped cat who likes to sleep under a big tree and pretend she is a real tiger. Sniffer is a gray cat who likes to sniff the flowers in Nikki's garden. Spot is a Dalmation with many black spots. Wiggles is a big furry brown dog who wiggles all over when he is happy.

1. Which dog is brown and furry? __Wiggles__
2. What color is Tiger? __orange with stripes__
3. What kind of dog is Spot? __Dalmation__
4. Which cat likes to sniff flowers? __Sniffer__
5. Where does Tiger like to sleep? __under a big tree__
6. Who wiggles all over when he is happy? __Wiggles__

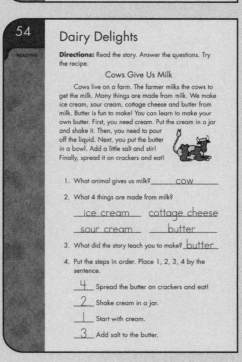

People on the Go — 53

Directions: Read the story about different kinds of transportation. Answer the questions with words from the story.

People use many kinds of transportation. Boats float on the water. Some people fish in a boat. Airplanes fly in the sky. Flying in a plane is a fast way to get somewhere. Trains run on a track. The first car is the engine. The last car is the caboose. Some people even sleep in beds on a train! A car has four wheels. Most people have a car. A car rides on roads. A bus can hold many people. A bus rides on roads. Most children ride a bus to school.

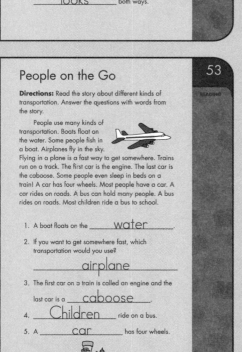

1. A boat floats on the __water__.
2. If you want to get somewhere fast, which transportation would you use? __airplane__
3. The first car on a train is called an engine and the last car is a __caboose__.
4. __Children__ ride on a bus.
5. A __car__ has four wheels.

Dairy Delights — 54

Directions: Read the story. Answer the questions. Try the recipe.

Cows Give Us Milk

Cows live on a farm. The farmer milks the cows to get the milk. Many things are made from milk. We make ice cream, sour cream, cottage cheese and butter from milk. Butter is fun to make! You can learn to make your own butter. First, you need cream. Put the cream in a jar and shake it. Then, you need to pour off the liquid. Next, you put the butter in a bowl. Add a little salt and stir! Finally, spread it on crackers and eat!

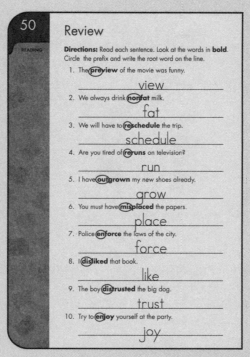

1. What animal gives us milk? __cow__
2. What 4 things are made from milk?
   __ice cream__   __cottage cheese__
   __sour cream__   __butter__
3. What did the story teach you to make? __butter__
4. Put the steps in order. Place 1, 2, 3, 4 by the sentence.
   __4__ Spread the butter on crackers and eat!
   __2__ Shake cream in a jar.
   __1__ Start with cream.
   __3__ Add salt to the butter.

232

Get the Story Straight

Spencer likes to make new friends. Today, he made friends with the dog in the picture.

Directions: Number the sentences in order to find out what Spencer did today.

__3__ Spencer kissed his mother good-bye.

__5__ Spencer saw the new dog next door.

__4__ Spencer went outside.

__6__ Spencer said hello.

__2__ Spencer got dressed and ate breakfast.

__1__ Spencer woke up.

Snacktime!

Alana and Marcus are hungry for a snack. They want to make nacho chips and cheese. The steps they need to follow are all mixed up.

Directions: Read the steps. Number them in 1, 2, 3 order. Then, color the picture.

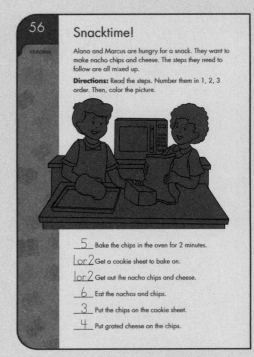

__5__ Bake the chips in the oven for 2 minutes.

__1or2__ Get a cookie sheet to bake on.

__1or2__ Get out the nacho chips and cheese.

__6__ Eat the nachos and chips.

__3__ Put the chips on the cookie sheet.

__4__ Put grated cheese on the chips.

Rain, Rain, Go Away

Directions: Read about rain. Then, follow the instructions.

Clouds are made up of little drops of ice and water. They push and bang into each other. Then, they join together to make bigger drops and begin to fall. More raindrops cling to them. They become heavy and fall quickly to the ground.

Write **first**, **second**, **third**, **fourth** and **fifth** to put the events in order.

__fourth__ More raindrops cling to them.

__first__ Clouds are made up of little drops of ice and water.

__third__ They join together and make bigger drops that begin to fall.

__second__ The drops of ice and water bang into each other.

__fifth__ The drops become heavy and fall quickly to the ground.

Follow Me

Directions: Read the sentences. Follow the instructions.

1. On Monday, Lisa needs bread. Use a **red** crayon to mark her path from her house to that building.

   Where does she go? __bakery__

2. On Tuesday, Lisa wants to read books. Use a green crayon to mark her path.

   Where does she go? __library__

3. On Wednesday, Lisa wants to swing. Use a yellow crayon to mark her path.

   Where does she go? __park__

4. On Thursday, Lisa wants to buy stamps. Use a **black** crayon to mark her path.

   Where does she go? __post office__

5. On Friday, Lisa wants to get money. Use a **purple** crayon to mark her path.

   Where does she go? __bank__

Map It!

Directions: Study the map of the United States. Follow the instructions.

Answers 1, 2 and 5 will vary.

1. Draw a star on the state where you live.
2. Draw a line from your state to the Atlantic Ocean.
3. Draw a triangle in the Gulf of Mexico.
4. Draw a circle in the Pacific Ocean.
5. Color each state that borders your state a different color.

CANADA

Pacific Ocean

Atlantic Ocean

Gulf of Mexico

N
W   E
S

Dare to Be Different

Directions: Look at the pictures. Draw an **X** on the picture in each row that is different.

Birds of a Feather
61 READING

Directions: Read about parrots and bluebirds. Then, complete the Venn diagram, telling how they are the same and different.

Bluebirds and parrots are both birds. Bluebirds and parrots can fly. They both have beaks. Parrots can live inside a cage. Bluebirds must live outdoors.

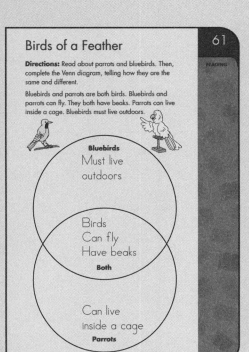

Bluebirds
Must live outdoors

Both
Birds
Can fly
Have beaks

Parrots
Can live inside a cage

Classifying Critters
62 READING

Directions: Use a **red** crayon to circle the names of three animals that would make good pets. Use a **blue** crayon to circle the names of three wild animals. Use an orange crayon to circle the two animals that live on a farm.

BEAR	CAT	LION	SHEEP
BIRD	DOG	COW	TIGER

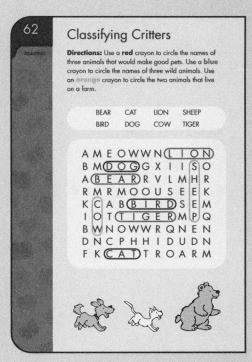

A M E O W W N (L I O N)
B M (D O G) G X I I S O
A (B E A R) R V L M H R
R M R M O O U S E E K
K C A B (B I R D) S E M
K I O T (T I G E R) M P Q
B W N O W W R Q N E N
D N C P H H I D U D N
F K (C A T) T R O A R M

Rainy Day Play
63 READING

Directions: Read the story. Then, circle the objects Jonathan needs to stay dry.

It is raining. Jonathan wants to play outdoors. What should he wear to stay dry? What should he carry to stay dry?

Art Smart
64 READING

Directions: Read about art tools. Then, color only the art tools.

Andrea uses different art tools to help her design her masterpieces. To cut, she needs scissors. To draw, she needs a pencil. To color, she needs crayons. To paint, she needs a brush.

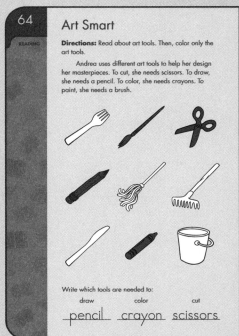

Write which tools are needed to:

draw   color   cut

pencil   crayon   scissors

Super Groups
65 READING

Directions: The words in each box form a group. Choose the word from the word box that describes each group and write it on the line.

clothes	family	noises	colors	flowers
fruits	animals	coins	toys	

rose	crash	mother
buttercup	bang	father
tulip	ring	sister
daisy	pop	brother
flowers	noises	family

puzzle	green	grapes
wagon	purple	orange
blocks	blue	apple
doll	red	plum
toys	colors	fruits

shirt	dime	dog
socks	penny	horse
dress	nickel	elephant
coat	quarter	moose
clothes	coins	animals

Tricky Tree
66 READING

This tricky tree has four different kinds of leaves: ash, poison ivy, silver maple and white oak.

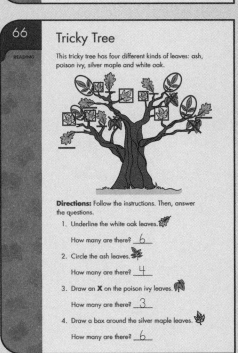

Directions: Follow the instructions. Then, answer the questions.

1. Underline the white oak leaves.

   How many are there? **6**

2. Circle the ash leaves.

   How many are there? **4**

3. Draw an **X** on the poison ivy leaves.

   How many are there? **3**

4. Draw a box around the silver maple leaves.

   How many are there? **6**

A Look at Ladybugs

67

Directions: Read about ladybugs. Then, answer the questions.

Have you ever seen a ladybug? Ladybugs are red. They have black spots. They have six legs. Ladybugs are pretty!

1. What color are ladybugs? __red__
2. What color are their spots? __black__
3. How many legs do ladybugs have? __six__

68

Paper Puppets

Directions: Read about paper-bag puppets. Then, follow the instructions.

It is easy to make a hand puppet. You need a small paper bag. You need colored paper. You need glue. You need scissors. Are you ready?

1. Circle the main idea:
   You need scissors.
   (Making a hand puppet is easy.)
2. Write the four objects you need to make a paper-bag puppet.
   1) __small paper bag__
   2) __colored paper__
   3) __glue__
   4) __scissors__
3. Draw a face on the paper-bag puppet.

Nice to Meet You

69

Directions: Read about how to meet a dog. Then, follow the instructions.

Do not try to pet a dog right away. First, let the dog sniff your hand. Do not move quickly. Do not talk loudly. Just let the dog sniff.

1. Predict what the dog will let you do if it likes you.
   __Pet it.__
2. What should you let the dog do?
   __Sniff your hand.__
3. Name three things you should not do when you meet a dog.
   1) __try to pet it__
   2) __move quickly__
   3) __talk loudly__

70

Sean Leads the Team

Directions: Read about Sean's basketball game. Then, answer the questions.

Sean really likes to play basketball. One sunny day, he decided to ask his friends to play basketball at the park, but there were six people—Sean, Aki, Lance, Kate, Zac and Oralia. A basketball team only allows five to play at a time. So, Sean decided to be the coach. Sean and his friends had fun.

1. How many kids wanted to play basketball? __six__
2. Write their names in ABC order:
   __Aki__
   __Kate__
   __Lance__
   __Oralia__
   __Sean__
   __Zac__

3. How many players can play on a basketball team at a time? __five__
4. Where did they play basketball? __at the park__
5. Who decided to be the coach? __Sean__

Rained Out

71

Predicting is telling what is likely to happen based on the facts.

Directions: Read the story. Then, check each sentence below that tells how the story could end.

One cloudy day, Juan and his baseball team, the Bears, played the Crocodiles. It was the last half of the fifth inning, and it started to rain. The coaches and umpires had to decide what to do.

✓ They kept playing until nine innings were finished.

✓ They ran for cover and waited until the rain stopped.

___ Each player grabbed an umbrella and returned to the field to finish the game.

✓ They canceled the game and played it another day.

___ They acted like crocodiles and slid around the wet bases.

___ The coaches played the game while the players sat in the dugout.

72

Dog-Gone!

Directions: Read the story. Then, follow the instructions.

Scotty and Simone were washing their dog, Willis. His fur was wet. Their hands were wet. Willis did NOT like to be wet. Scotty dropped the soap. Simone picked it up and let go of Willis. Uh-oh!

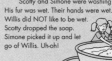

1. Write what happened next.
   __Answers will vary.__

2. Draw what happened next.

Drawings will vary.

Game Time!

73 READING

A **fact** is something that can be proven. An **opinion** is a feeling or belief about something and cannot be proven.

Directions: Read these sentences about different games. Then, write **F** next to each fact and **O** next to each opinion.

O 1. Tennis is cool!

F 2. There are red and black markers in a Checkers game.

F 3. In football, a touchdown is worth six points.

O 4. Being a goalie in soccer is easy.

F 5. A yo-yo moves on a string.

O 6. June's sister looks like the queen on the card.

F 7. The six kids need three more players for a baseball team.

O 8. Table tennis is more fun than court tennis.

Owls Are a Hoot

74 READING

Directions: Read the story. Then, follow the instructions.

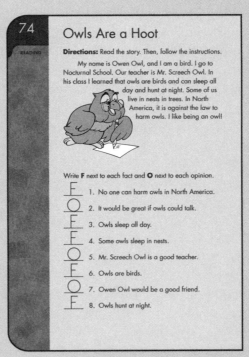

My name is Owen Owl, and I am a bird. I go to Nocturnal School. Our teacher is Mr. Screech Owl. In his class I learned that owls are birds and can sleep all day and hunt at night. Some of us live in nests in trees. In North America, it is against the law to harm owls. I like being an owl!

Write **F** next to each fact and **O** next to each opinion.

F 1. No one can harm owls in North America.

O 2. It would be great if owls could talk.

F 3. Owls sleep all day.

F 4. Some owls sleep in nests.

O 5. Mr. Screech Owl is a good teacher.

F 6. Owls are birds.

O 7. Owen Owl would be a good friend.

F 8. Owls hunt at night.

Chef Jeff

75 READING

Directions: Read the story. Then, answer the questions.

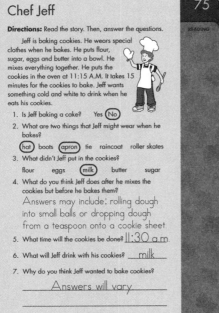

Jeff is baking cookies. He wears special clothes when he bakes. He puts flour, sugar, eggs and butter into a bowl. He mixes everything together. He puts the cookies in the oven at 11:15 A.M. It takes 15 minutes for the cookies to bake. Jeff wants something cold and white to drink when he eats his cookies.

1. Is Jeff baking a cake?   Yes   (No)

2. What are two things that Jeff might wear when he bakes?
   (hat)   boots   (apron)   tie   raincoat   roller skates

3. What didn't Jeff put in the cookies?
   flour   eggs   (milk)   butter   sugar

4. What do you think Jeff does after he mixes the cookies but before he bakes them?
   Answers may include: rolling dough into small balls or dropping dough from a teaspoon onto a cookie sheet.

5. What time will the cookies be done? 11:30 a.m.

6. What will Jeff drink with his cookies? milk

7. Why do you think Jeff wanted to bake cookies?
   Answers will vary.

Mother's Helper

76 READING

Directions: Read more about sea horses. Then, answer the questions.

A father sea horse helps the mother. He has a small sack or pouch, on the front of his body. The mother sea horse lays the eggs. She does not keep them. She gives the eggs to the father.

1. What does the mother sea horse do with her eggs?
   She gives them to the father.

2. Where does the father sea horse put the eggs?
   in his pouch

3. Sea horses can change color. Color the sea horses.

What Do You See?

77 READING

Directions: Read this story about Ling and Bradley. Draw pictures for the beginning and middle to describe each part of the story.

Beginning: One sunny day, Ling and Bradley, wearing their empty backpacks, rode their bikes down the street to the park.

Drawings will vary.

Middle: They stopped by an oak tree with many acorns under it. They picked up some and stuffed them into their backpacks.

Drawings will vary.

Directions: Draw an ending for this story that tells what you think they did with the acorns.

End: With the heavy backpacks strapped on their backs, they pedaled home.

Drawings will vary.

It's No Problem!

78 READING

Juniper has three problems to solve. She needs your help.

Directions: Read each problem. Write what you think she should do.

1. Juniper is watching her favorite TV show when the power goes out.
   Answers will vary.

2. Juniper is riding her bike to school when the front tire goes flat.
   Answers will vary.

3. Juniper loses her father while shopping in the supermarket.
   Answers will vary.

Picture This
79

Directions: Draw three pictures to tell a story about each topic.

1. Feeding a pet

Beginning

Drawings will vary.

Middle

Drawings will vary.

End

Drawings will vary.

2. Playing with a friend

Beginning

Drawings will vary.

Middle

Drawings will vary.

End

Drawings will vary.

Bookworms
80

Directions: Use the clues to help the children find their books. Draw a line from each child's name to the correct book.

Brett   Aki   Lorenzo   Kate   Zac   Oralia

CHILDREN

Brett
Aki
Lorenzo
Kate
Zac
Oralia

BOOKS

jokes
cakes
monsters
games
flags
space

Brett → games
Aki → monsters
Lorenzo → jokes
Kate → cakes
Zac → flags
Oralia → space

Clues

1. Lorenzo likes jokes.
2. Kate likes to bake.
3. Oralia likes far away places.
4. Aki does not like monsters or flags.
5. Zac does not like space or monsters.
6. Brett does not like games, jokes or cakes.

What's for Dinner?
81

Dad is cooking dinner tonight. You can find out what day of the week it is.

Directions: Read the clues. Complete the menu. Answer the question.

Menu

Monday	pizza
Tuesday	chicken
Wednesday	corn-on-the-cob
Thursday	meat pie
Friday	hot dogs
Saturday	fish
Sunday	cheese rolls

1. Mom fixed pizza on Monday.
2. Dad fixed cheese rolls the day before that.
3. Tess made meat pie three days after Mom fixed pizza.
4. Tom fixed corn-on-the-cob the day before Tess made meat pie.
5. Mom fixed hot dogs the day after Tess made meat pie.
6. Tess cooked fish the day before Dad fixed cheese rolls.
7. Dad is making chicken today. What day is it?

   Tuesday

Review
82

Directions: Read the story. Then, answer the questions.

Randa, Emily, Ali, Dave, Liesl and Deana all love to read. Every Tuesday, they all go to the library together and pick out their favorite books. Randa likes books about fish. Emily likes books about sports and athletes. Ali likes books about art. Dave likes books about wild animals. Liesl likes books with riddles and puzzles. Deanna likes books about cats and dogs.

1. Circle the main idea:

   Randa, Emily, Ali, Dave, Liesl and Deana are good friends.

   (Randa, Emily, Ali, Dave, Liesl and Deana all like books.)

2. Who do you think might grow up to be an artist?

   Ali

3. Who do you think might grow up to be an oceanographer (someone who studies the ocean)?

   Randa

4. Who do you think might grow up to be a veterinarian (an animal doctor)?

   Deanna

5. Who do you think might grow up to be a zookeeper (someone who cares for zoo animals)?

   Dave

Twister Tips
83

Directions: Read about tornadoes. Then, follow the instructions.

A tornado begins over land with strong winds and thunderstorms. The spinning air becomes a funnel. It can cause damage. If you are inside, go to the lowest floor of the building. A basement is a safe place. A bathroom or closet in the middle of a building can be a safe place, too. If you are outside, lie in a ditch. Remember, tornadoes are dangerous.

Write five facts about tornadoes.

1. A tornado begins over land
2. Spinning air becomes a funnel
3. Tornadoes can cause damage
4. A basement is a safe place to be in a tornado
5. If you are outside during a tornado, you should lie in a ditch.

What a Breeze!
84

The setting is where a story takes place. The characters are the people in a story or play.

Directions: Read about Hercules. Then, answer the questions.

Hercules was born in the warm Atlantic Ocean. He was a very small and weak baby. He wanted to be the strongest hurricane in the world. But he had one problem. He couldn't blow 75-mile-per-hour winds. Hercules blew and blew in the ocean, until one day, his sister, Hola, told him it would be more fun to be a breeze than a hurricane. Hercules agreed. It was a breeze to be a breeze!

1. What is the setting of the story?

   Atlantic Ocean

2. Who are the characters?

   Hercules, Hola

3. What is the problem?

   Hercules couldn't blow 75 mile-per-hour winds.

4. How does Hercules solve his problem?

   He decides that it is more fun to be a breeze than a hurricane

Red, White, and Blue · 85

Directions: Read each story. Then, write whether it is fiction or nonfiction.

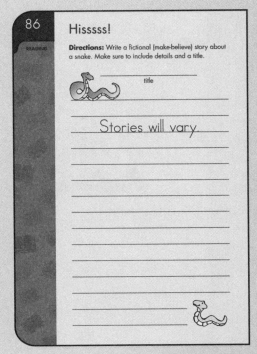

One sunny day in July, a dog named Stan ran away from home. He went up one street and down the other looking for fun, but all the yards were empty. Where was everybody? Stan kept walking until he heard the sound of band music and happy people. Stan walked faster until he got to Central Street. There he saw men, women, children and dogs getting ready to walk in a parade. It was the Fourth of July!

Fiction or Nonfiction? **Fiction**

Americans celebrate the Fourth of July every year, because it is the birthday of the United States of America. On July 4, 1776, the United States got its independence from Great Britain. Today, Americans celebrate this holiday with parades, picnics and fireworks as they proudly wave the red, white and blue American flag.

Fiction or Nonfiction? **Nonfiction**

86 · Hisssss!

Directions: Write a fictional (make-believe) story about a snake. Make sure to include details and a title.

_____ title

Stories will vary.

88 · Know Your ABCs

Directions: Write these words in order. If two words start with the same letter, look at the second letter in each word.

Example: lamb Lamb comes first because **a** comes **light** before **i** in the alphabet.

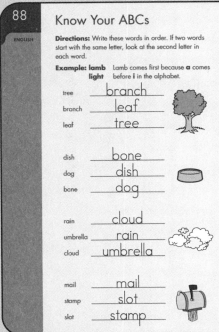

tree — **branch**
branch — **leaf**
leaf — **tree**

dish — **bone**
dog — **dish**
bone — **dog**

rain — **cloud**
umbrella — **rain**
cloud — **umbrella**

mail — **mail**
stamp — **slot**
slot — **stamp**

From A to Z · 89

If the first letters of two words are the same, look at the second letters in both words. If the second letters are the same, look at the third letters.

Directions: Write 1, 2, 3 or 4 on the lines in each row to put the words in ABC order.

Example:

1. **1** candy **2** carrot **4** duck **3** dance
2. **2** cold **4** hot **1** carry **3** hit
3. **2** flash **1** fan **3** fun **4** garden
4. **2** seat **4** sun **1** saw **3** sit
5. **3** row **1** ring **2** rock **4** run
6. **2** truck **3** turn **4** twin **1** talk

90 · Friends and Family

Directions: Write the following names in ABC order: Oscar, Ali, Lance, Kim, Zane and Bonita.

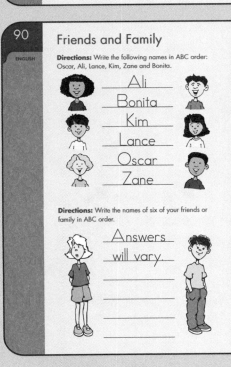

Ali
Bonita
Kim
Lance
Oscar
Zane

Directions: Write the names of six of your friends or family in ABC order.

Answers will vary.

Super Similar · 91

Words that mean the same or nearly the same are called **synonyms**.

Directions: Read the sentence that tells about the picture. Draw a circle around the word that means the same as the **bold** word.

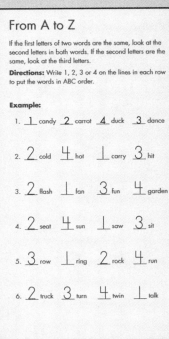

The child is **unhappy**. (sad) hungry

The flowers are **lovely**. (pretty) green

The baby was very **tired**. (sleepy) hurt

The **funny** clown made us laugh. (silly) glad

The ladybug is so **tiny**. (small) red

We saw a **scary** tiger. (frightening) ugly

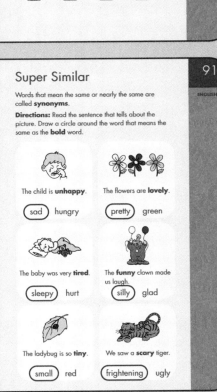

92 A Silly Synonym Story

Synonyms are words that have almost the same meaning.

Directions: Read the story. Then, fill in the blanks with the synonyms.

funny   unhappy
windy   little

A New Balloon

It was a breezy day. The wind blew the small child's balloon away. The child was sad. A silly clown gave him a new balloon.

1. It was a __windy__ day.
2. The wind blew the __little__ child's balloon away.
3. The child was __unhappy__.
4. A __funny__ clown gave him a new balloon.

93 So Many Synonyms!

Directions: Read each sentence. Fill in the blanks with the synonyms.

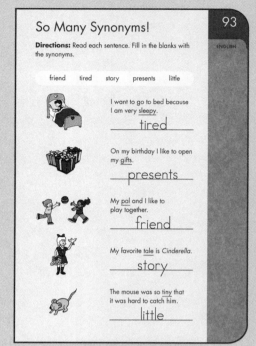

friend   tired   story   presents   little

I want to go to bed because I am very sleepy.
__tired__

On my birthday I like to open my gifts.
__presents__

My pal and I like to play together.
__friend__

My favorite tale is *Cinderella*.
__story__

The mouse was so tiny that it was hard to catch him.
__little__

94 All About Antonyms

Antonyms are words that mean the opposite of another word.

Examples:
hot and **cold**
short and **tall**

Directions: Draw a line from each word on the left to its antonym on the right.

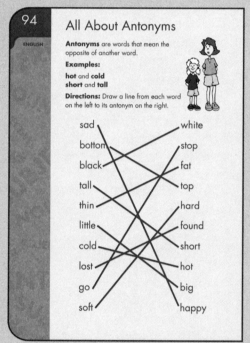

sad — happy
bottom — top
black — white
tall — short
thin — fat
little — big
cold — hot
lost — found
go — stop
soft — hard

95 Spotty on the Go

Directions: Read the sentences. Complete each sentence with the correct antonym. Use the clues in the picture and below each sentence. Then, color the picture.

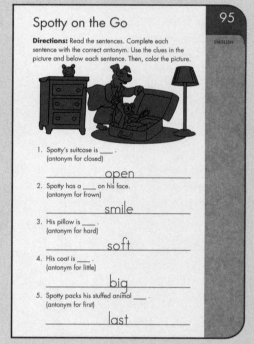

1. Spotty's suitcase is ____ .
   (antonym for closed)
   __open__
2. Spotty has a ____ on his face.
   (antonym for frown)
   __smile__
3. His pillow is ____ .
   (antonym for hard)
   __soft__
4. His coat is ____ .
   (antonym for little)
   __big__
5. Spotty packs his stuffed animal ____ .
   (antonym for first)
   __last__

96 Hearing Homophones

Homophones are words that sound the same but are spelled differently and mean different things.

Directions: Write the homophone from the box next to each picture.

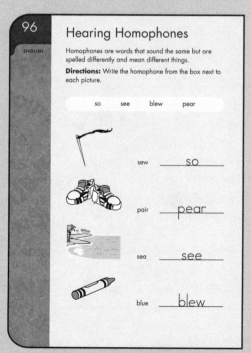

so   see   blew   pear

sew __so__

pair __pear__

sea __see__

blue __blew__

97 Which One's Which?

Directions: Look at each picture. Circle the correct homophone.

(deer)   dear   blue   (blew)

(two)   to   hi   (high)

by   (bye)   (new)   knew

98 Nouns I Know

A noun is the name of a person, place or thing.

Directions: Read the story and circle all the nouns. Then, write the nouns next to the pictures below.

Our family likes to go to the park. — family / park

We play on the swings. — swings

We eat cake. — cake

We drink lemonade. — lemonade

We throw the ball to our dog. — ball / dog

Then, we go home. — home

99 Nouns All Around

Directions: Look through a magazine. Cut out pictures of nouns and glue them below. Write the name of the noun next to the picture.

Nouns

Answers will vary.

100 Name-It Nouns

Proper nouns are the names of specific people, places and pets. Proper nouns begin with a capital letter.

Directions: Write the proper nouns on the lines below. Use capital letters at the beginning of each word.

logan, utah — Logan, Utah

mike smith — Mike Smith

lynn cramer — Lynn Cramer

buster — Buster

fluffy — Fluffy

chicago, illinois — Chicago, Illinois

101 It's a Date!

The days of the week and the months of the year are always capitalized.

Directions: Circle the words that are written correctly. Write the words that need capital letters on the lines below.

sunday, (July), (Wednesday)
may, december, friday
tuesday, june, august
(Monday), january, (February)
(March), (Thursday), (April)
(September), saturday, (October)

Days of the Week
1. Sunday
2. Friday
3. Tuesday
4. Saturday

Months of the Year
1. January
2. June
3. May
4. August
5. December

102 A Capital Idea

The first word and all of the important words in a title begin with a capital letter.

Directions: Write the book titles on the lines below. Use capital letters.

1. Dinosaurs
2. Lizards Everywhere
3. The Magic Cat
4. All About Presidents
5. The Space Dog
6. Gerbil Care

103 A Number of Nouns

Plural nouns name more than one person, place or thing.

Directions: Read the words in the box. Write the words in the correct column.

hats, girl, cows, kittens, cake
poons, glass, book, horse, trees

one | more than one

girl — hats
glass — spoons
book — cows
horse — kittens
cake — trees

Plenty of Plurals

Plurals are words that mean more than one. You usually add an **s** or **es** to the word. In some words ending in **y**, the **y** changes to an **i** before adding **es**. For example, **baby** changes to **babies**.

Directions: Look at the following lists of plural words. Write the word that means one next to it. The first one has been done for you.

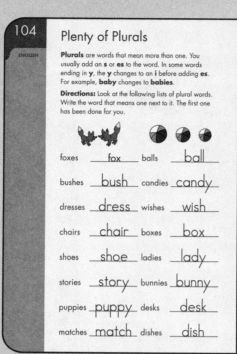

foxes	fox	balls	ball
bushes	bush	candies	candy
dresses	dress	wishes	wish
chairs	chair	boxes	box
shoes	shoe	ladies	lady
stories	story	bunnies	bunny
puppies	puppy	desks	desk
matches	match	dishes	dish

Pronoun Pros

Pronouns are words that can be used instead of nouns. **She**, **he**, **it** and **they** are pronouns.

Directions: Read the sentence. Then, write the sentence again, using **she**, **he**, **it** or **they** in the blank.

1. Dan likes funny jokes.
   _He_ likes funny jokes.

2. Peg and Sam went to the zoo.
   They went to the zoo.

3. My dog likes to dig in the yard.
   _It_ likes to dig in the yard.

4. Sara is a very good dancer.
   She is a very good dancer.

5. Fred and Ted are twins.
   They are twins.

What's It All About?

The **subject** of a sentence is the person, place or thing the sentence is about.

Directions: Underline the subject in each sentence.

Example: Mom read a book.
(Think: Who is the sentence about? Mom)

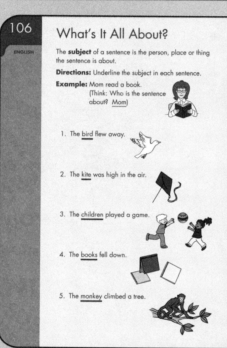

1. The bird flew away.

2. The kite was high in the air.

3. The children played a game.

4. The books fell down.

5. The monkey climbed a tree.

Double Up

Two similar sentences can be joined into one sentence if the predicate is the same. A **compound subject** is made up of two subjects joined together by the word **and**.

Example: Jamie can sing.
Sandy can sing.
Jamie **and** Sandy can sing.

Directions: Combine the sentences. Write the new sentence on the line.

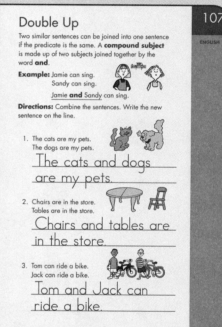

1. The cats are my pets.
   The dogs are my pets.
   The cats and dogs are my pets.

2. Chairs are in the store.
   Tables are in the store.
   Chairs and tables are in the store.

3. Tom can ride a bike.
   Jack can ride a bike.
   Tom and Jack can ride a bike.

Play Ball!

A **verb** is the action word in a sentence. Verbs tell what something does or that something exists.

Example: Run, sleep and jump are verbs.

Directions: Circle the verbs in the sentences below.

1. We (play) baseball everyday.

2. Susan (pitches) the ball very well.

3. Mike (swings) the bat harder than anyone.

4. Chris (slides) into home base.

5. Laura (hit) a home run.

Verb Alert!

We use verbs to tell when something happens. Sometimes we add an **ed** to verbs that tell us if something has already happened.

Example: Today, we will **play**. Yesterday, we **played**.

Directions: Write the correct verb in the blank.

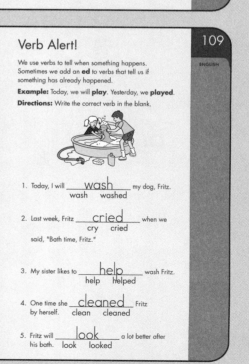

1. Today, I will _wash_ my dog, Fritz.
   wash   washed

2. Last week, Fritz _cried_ when we
   cry   cried
   said, "Bath time, Fritz."

3. My sister likes to _help_ wash Fritz.
   help   helped

4. One time she _cleaned_ Fritz
   by herself.   clean   cleaned

5. Fritz will _look_ a lot better after
   his bath.   look   looked

110 Predicate Power

The **predicate** is the part of the sentence that tells about the action.

Directions: Circle the predicate in each sentence.

Example: The boys ran on the playground.
(Think: The boys did what? (Ran))

1. The woman (painted) a picture.

2. The puppy (chases) his ball.

3. The students (went) to school.

4. Butterflies (fly) in the air.

5. The baby (wants) a drink.

111 Twice the Action

A **compound predicate** is made by joining two sentences that have the same subject. The predicates are joined together by the word **and**.

Example: Tom can jump.
Tom can run.
Tom can run **and** jump.

Directions: Combine the sentences. Write the new sentence on the line.

1. The dog can roll over.
The dog can bark.

   The dog can roll over and bark.

2. My mom plays with me.
My mom reads with me.

   My mom plays and reads with me.

3. Tara is tall.
Tara is smart.

   Tara is tall and smart.

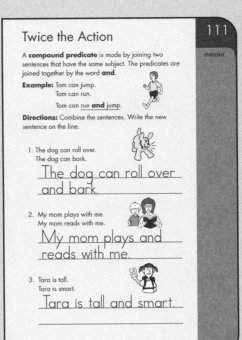

112 School Days

The **subject** part of the sentence is the person, place or thing the sentence is about. The **predicate** is the part of the sentence that tells what the subject does.

Directions: Draw a line between the subject and the predicate. Underline the noun in the subject and circle the verb.

Example: The furry <u>cat</u> | (ate) food.

1. <u>Mandi</u> | (walks) to school.

2. The <u>bus</u> | (drove) the children.

3. The school <u>bell</u> | (rang) very loudly.

4. The <u>teacher</u> | (spoke) to the students.

5. The <u>girls</u> | (opened) their books.

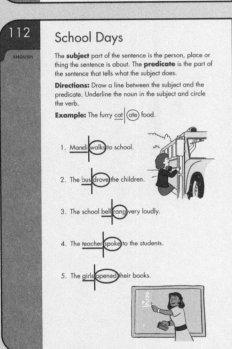

113 All Together Now

Directions: Write one new sentence using a compound subject or predicate.

Example: The boy will jump. The girl will jump.
The <u>boy and girl</u> will jump.

1. The clowns run. The clowns play.

   The clowns run and play.

2. The dogs dance. The bears dance.

   The dogs and bears dance.

3. Seals bark. Seals clap.

   Seals bark and clap.

4. The girls play. The girls laugh.

   The girls play and laugh.

114 Ready to Roll

Directions: Draw a circle around the noun, the naming part of the sentence. Draw a line under the verb, the action part of the sentence.

Example: (John) <u>drinks</u> juice every morning.

1. Our (class) <u>skates</u> at the roller-skating rink.

2. (Miguel) and (Emma) <u>go</u> very fast.

3. (Austin) <u>eats</u> hot dogs.

4. (Sierra) <u>dances</u> to the music.

5. (Everyone) <u>likes</u> the skating rink.

115 Tell Me More!

Adjectives are words that tell more about a person, place or thing.

Examples: cold, fuzzy, dark

Directions: Circle the adjectives in the sentences.

1. The (juicy) apple is on the plate.

2. The (furry) dog is eating a bone.

3. It was a (sunny) day.

4. The kitten drinks (warm) milk.

5. The baby has a (loud) cry.

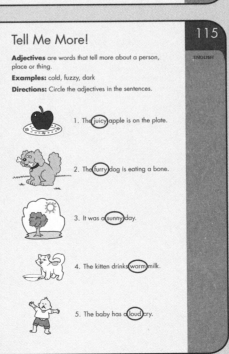

242

ANSWER KEY

116 | A Day on the Farm

Directions: Choose an adjective from the box to fill in the blanks.

hungry	sunny	busy	funny
fresh	deep	pretty	cloudy

1. It is a __sunny__ day on Farmer Brown's farm.

2. Farmer Brown is a very __busy__ man.

3. Mrs. Brown likes to feed the __hungry__ chickens.

4. Every day she collects the __fresh__ eggs.

5. The ducks swim in the __deep__ pond.

117 | Make a Wish!

Articles are small words that help us to better understand nouns. **A** and **an** are articles. We use **an** before a word that begins with a vowel. We use **a** before **a** word that begins with a consonant.

Example: We looked in **a** nest. It had **an** eagle in it.

Directions: Read the sentences. Write **a** or **an** in the blank.

1. 1. I found __a__ book.

2. It had a story about __an__ ant in it.

3. In the story, __a__ lion gave three wishes to ant.

4. The ant's first wish was to ride __an__ elephant.

5. The second wish was to ride __an__ alligator.

6. The last wish was __a__ wish for three more wishes.

118 | Sentence Sense

A **sentence** tells a complete idea. It has a noun and a verb. It begins with a capital letter and has punctuation at the end.

Directions: Circle the group of words if it is a sentence.

1. (Grass is a green plant.)

2. Mowing the lawn.

3. (Grass grows in fields and lawns.)

4. Tickle the feet.

5. (Sheep, cows and horses eat grass.)

6. We like to play in.

7. (My sister likes to mow the lawn.)

8. A picnic on the grass.

119 | Making a Statement

Statements are sentences that tell us something. They begin with a capital letter and end with a period.

Directions: Write the sentences on the lines below. Begin each sentence with a capital letter and end it with a period.

1. we like to ride our bikes
   We like to ride our bikes.

2. we go down the hill very fast
   We go down the hill very fast.

3. we keep our bikes shiny and clean
   We keep our bikes shiny and clean.

4. we know how to change the tires
   We know how to change the tires.

120 | Ask Me a Question

Questions are sentences that ask something. They begin with a capital letter and end with a question mark.

Directions: Write the questions on the lines below. Begin each sentence with a capital letter and end it with a question mark.

1. will you be my friend
   Will you be my friend?

2. what is your name
   What is your name?

3. are you eight years old
   Are you eight years old?

4. do you like rainbows
   Do you like rainbows?

121 | What a Surprise!

Surprising sentences tell a strong feeling and end with an exclamation point. A surprising sentence may be only one or two words showing fear, surprise or pain.

Example: Oh, no!

Directions: Put a period at the end of the sentences that tell something. Put an exclamation point at the end of the sentences that tell a strong feeling. Put a question mark at the end of the sentences that ask a question.

1. The cheetah can run very fast.

2. Wow!

3. Look at that cheetah go!

4. Can you run fast?

5. Oh, my!

6. You're faster than I am.

7. Let's run together.

8. We can run as fast as a cheetah.

9. What fun!

10. Do you think cheetahs get tired?

---

122 ENGLISH

That's Mine!

We add **'s** to nouns (people, places or things) to tell who or what owns something.

Directions: Read the sentences. Fill in the blanks to show ownership.

Example: The doll belongs to **Sara**.
It is **Sara's** doll.

1. Sparky has a red collar.
   __Sparky's__ collar is red.

2. Jimmy has a blue coat.
   __Jimmy's__ coat is blue.

3. The tail of the cat is short.
   The __cat's__ tail is short.

4. The name of my mother is Karen.
   My __mother's__ name is Karen.

---

123 ENGLISH

Owning Up

Directions: Read the sentences. Choose the correct word and write it in the sentences below.

1. The __boy's__ lunchbox is broken.
   boys   boy's

2. The __gerbils__ played in the cage.
   gerbil's   gerbils

3. __Ann's__ hair is brown.
   Anns   Ann's

4. The __horses__ ran in the field.
   horse's   horses

5. My __sister's__ coat is torn.
   sister's   sisters

6. The __cat's__ fur is brown.
   cats   cat's

7. Three __birds__ flew past our window.
   birds   bird's

8. The __dog's__ paws are muddy.
   dogs   dog's

---

124 ENGLISH

Look It Up

A dictionary is a book that gives the meaning of words. It also tells how words sound. Words in a dictionary are in ABC order. That makes them easier to find. A picture dictionary lists a word, a picture of the word and its meaning.

Directions: Look at this page from a picture dictionary. Then, answer the questions.

baby
A very young child.

band
A group of people who play music.

bank
A place where money is kept.

bark
The sound a dog makes.

berry
A small, juicy fruit.

board
A flat piece of wood.

1. What is a small, juicy fruit? __berry__
2. What is a group of people who play music? __band__
3. What is the name for a very young child? __baby__
4. What is a flat piece of wood called? __board__

---

125 ENGLISH

Word to Word

The guide words at the top of a page in a dictionary tell you what the first and last words on the page will be. Only words that come in ABC order between those two words will be on that page. Guide words help you find the page you need to look up a word.

Directions: Write each word from the box in ABC order between each pair of guide words.

| faint | far | fence | feed | farmer |
| fan | feet | farm | family | face |

face   **fence**

few	first
fierce	fish
fight	fix
fill	flat
finish	flush

---

126 ENGLISH

Many Meanings

When words have more than one meaning, the meanings are numbered in a dictionary.

Directions: Read the meanings of **tag**. Write the number of the correct definition after each sentence.

tag
1. A small strip or tab attached to something else.
2. To label.
3. To follow closely and constantly.
4. A game of chase.

1. We will play a game of tag after we study. __4__
2. I will tag this coat with its price. __2__
3. My little brother will tag along with us. __3__
4. My mother already took off the price tag. __1__
5. The tag on the puppy said, "For Sale." __1__
6. Do not tag that tree. __2__

---

128 SPELLING

Number Names

Directions: Write each number word beside the correct picture. Then, write it again.

Example: __six   six__

| one two three four five six seven eight nine ten |

 __one   one__

 __three   three__

 __two   two__

 __nine   nine__

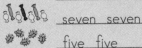 __four   four__

__seven   seven__

__five   five__

__ten   ten__

__eight   eight__

Say It With Numbers

129

Directions: Change the telling sentences into asking sentences. Change the asking sentences into telling sentences. Begin each one with a capital letter and end it with a period or a question mark.

Examples:

Is she eating three cookies?

She is eating three cookies.

He is bringing one truck.

Is he bringing one truck?

1. Is he painting two bluebirds?

He is painting two bluebirds.

2. Did she find four apples?

She did find four apples.

3. She will be six on her birthday.

She will be six on her birthday.

130

Super Sounds: Short a

Directions: Use a word from the box to complete each sentence.

fat	path	lamp	can
van	stamp	Dan	math
sat	cat	fan	bat

Example:

1. The _____lamp_____ had a pink shade.

2. The bike _____path_____ led us to the park.

3. I like to add in _____math_____ class.

4. The cat is very _____fat_____.

5. The _____can_____ of beans was hard to open.

6. The envelope needed a _____stamp_____.

7. He swung the _____bat_____ and hit the ball.

8. The _____fan_____ blew air around.

9. My mom drives a blue _____van_____.

10. I _____sat_____ in the backseat.

Super Sounds: Long a

131

Long a is the vowel sound which says its own name. **Long a** can be spelled **ai** as in the word **mail**, **ay** as in the word **say** and **a** with a **silent e** at the end of a word as in the word **same**.

Directions: Say each word and listen for the **long a** sound. Then, write each word and underline the letters that make the **long a** vowel sound.

mail	bake	train
game	day	sale
paint	play	name
made	gray	tray

1. mail
2. paint
3. game
4. made
5. bake
6. play

7. day
8. gray
9. train
10. name
11. sale
12. tray

132

Super Sounds: Short e

Directions: Write the correct short e word in each sentence.

get	Meg	rest	bed	spent
test	head	pet	red	best

1. Of all my crayons, I like the _____red_____ color the _____best_____.

2. I always make my _____bed_____ when I _____get_____ up.

3. My new hat keeps my _____head_____ warm.

4. _____Meg_____ wanted a dog for a _____pet_____.

5. I have a _____test_____ in math tomorrow, so I want to get a good night's _____sleep_____.

Super Sounds: Long e

133

Long e is the vowel sound which says its own name. **Long e** can be spelled **ee** as in the word **teeth**, **ea** as in the word **meat** or **e** as in the word **me**.

Directions: Say each word and listen for the **long e** sound. Then, write the words and underline the letters that make the **long e** sound.

street	neat	treat
feet	sleep	keep
deal	meal	mean
clean	beast	feast

1. street
2. sleep
3. mean
4. neat
5. keep
6. clean

7. treat
8. deal
9. beast
10. feet
11. meal
12. feast

134

Super Sounds: Short i

Short i is the sound you hear in the word **pin**.

Directions: Use the **short i** words in the box to write rhyming words.

pin	fin	win	fish
pitch	wish	rich	kick
ship	dip	dish	sick

1. Write the words that rhyme with **spin**.

pin   fin   win

2. Write the words that rhyme with **ditch**.

pitch   rich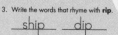

3. Write the words that rhyme with **rip**.

ship   dip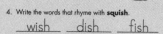

4. Write the words that rhyme with **squish**.

wish   dish   fish

5. Write the words that rhyme with **lick**.

kick   sick

Super Sounds: Long i 135

Long i is the vowel sound which says its own name. **Long i** can be spelled **igh** as in **sight**, **i** with a **silent e** at the end as in **mine** and **y** at the end as in **fly**.

Directions: Say each word and listen for the **long i** sound. Then, write each word and underline the letters that make the **long i** sound.

bike	hike	ride
line	glide	ripe
nine	pipe	fight
high	light	sigh

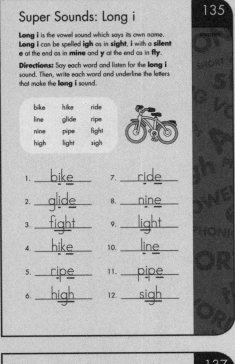

1. <u>bike</u>
2. <u>glide</u>
3. <u>fight</u>
4. <u>hike</u>
5. <u>ripe</u>
6. <u>high</u>
7. <u>ride</u>
8. <u>nine</u>
9. <u>light</u>
10. <u>line</u>
11. <u>pipe</u>
12. <u>sigh</u>

Super Sounds: Short o 136

Short o is the vowel sound you hear in the word **got**.

Directions: Use the **short o** words in the box to write rhyming words.

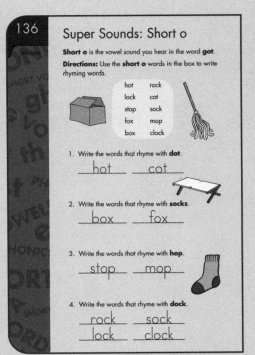

hot	rock
lock	cot
stop	sock
fox	mop
box	clock

1. Write the words that rhyme with **dot**.

   hot   cot

2. Write the words that rhyme with **socks**.

   box   fox

3. Write the words that rhyme with **hop**.

   stop   mop

4. Write the words that rhyme with **dock**.

   rock   sock
   lock   clock

Super Sounds: Long o 137

Directions: Draw a line from the first part of the sentence to the part which completes the sentence.

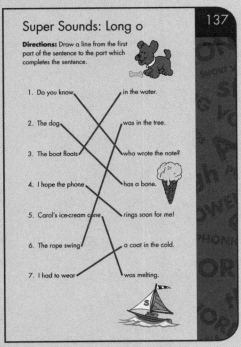

1. Do you know — who wrote the note?
2. The dog — has a bone.
3. The boat floats — in the water.
4. I hope the phone — rings soon for me!
5. Carol's ice-cream cone — was melting.
6. The rope swing — was in the tree.
7. I had to wear — a coat in the cold.

Super Sounds: Short u 138

Directions: Circle the words in each sentence which are not correct. Then, write the correct **short u** words from the box on the lines.

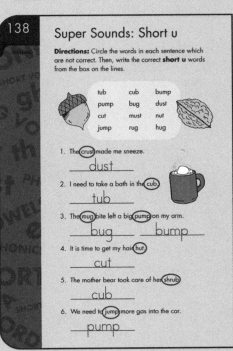

tub	cub	bump
pump	bug	dust
cut	must	nut
jump	rug	hug

1. The (crust) made me sneeze.

   dust

2. I need to take a bath in the (cub).

   tub

3. The (mug) bite left a big (pump) on my arm.

   bug   bump

4. It is time to get my hair (hut).

   cut

5. The mother bear took care of her (shrub).

   cub

6. We need to (jump) more gas into the car.

   pump

Super Sounds: Long u 139

Long u is the vowel sound you hear in the word **cube**. Another vowel sound which is very much like the **long u** sound is the **oo** sound you hear in the word **boot**.

Directions: Use the **long u** and **oo** words in the box to write rhyming words.

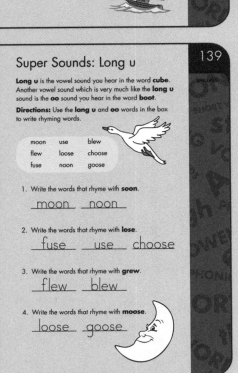

moon	use	blew
flew	loose	choose
fuse	noon	goose

1. Write the words that rhyme with **soon**.

   moon   noon

2. Write the words that rhyme with **lose**.

   fuse   use   choose

3. Write the words that rhyme with **grew**.

   flew   blew

4. Write the words that rhyme with **moose**.

   loose   goose

Ready, Set, Action! 140

Verbs are words that tell the action in the sentence.

Directions: Draw a line from each sentence to its picture. Then, finish the sentence with the verb or action word that is under each picture.

Example:

He will <u>help</u> the baby.

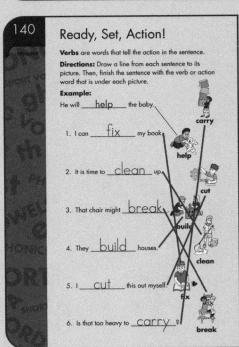

1. I can <u>fix</u> my book.

   carry

2. It is time to <u>clean</u> up.

   help

3. That chair might <u>break</u>.

   cut

4. They <u>build</u> houses.

   build

5. I <u>cut</u> this out myself.

   clean

6. Is that too heavy to <u>carry</u>?

   fix

   break

246

How Does It End? 141

Most **verbs** end with **s** when the sentence tells about one thing. The **s** is taken away when the sentence tells about more than one thing.

Example:

One dog walks.   One boy runs.
Two dogs **walk**.   Three boys **run**.

The spelling of some **verbs** changes when the sentence tells about only one thing.

One girl carries her lunch.   The boy fixes his car.
Two girls **carry** their lunches.   The boys **fix** their cars.

Directions: Write the missing verbs in the sentences.

Example:

Pam works hard. She and Peter ___work___ all day.

1. The father bird builds a nest.

   The mother and father ___build___ it together.

2. The girls clean their room.

   Jenny ___cleans___ under her bed.

3. The children cut out their pictures.

   Henry ___cuts___ his slowly.

4. These workers fix things.

   This man ___fixes___ televisions.

5. Two trucks carry horses.

   One truck ___carries___ pigs.

---

142 Animal Action

Directions: Circle the word in each sentence that is not spelled correctly. Then, write it correctly.

| squirrel | bears | rabbit | deer | fox | mouse |

Example:
Animals like to live in (threes)   ___trees___

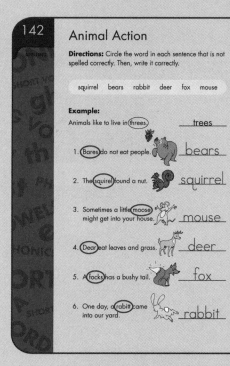

1. (Bares) do not eat people.   ___bears___

2. The (squirl) found a nut.   ___squirrel___

3. Sometimes a little (moose) might get into your house.   ___mouse___

4. (Dear) eat leaves and grass.   ___deer___

5. A (focks) has a bushy tail.   ___fox___

6. One day, a (rabbitt) came into our yard.   ___rabbit___

Lots of Animals 143

Directions: Write the two sentences below as one sentence. Remember the special spelling of **fox**, **mouse** and **deer** when there are more than one.

Example:

I saw a mouse. You saw a mouse.

___We saw two mice.___

1. Julie petted a deer.
   Matt petted a deer.

   ___Julie and Matt petted___
   ___a deer.___

2. Mike colored a fox.
   Kim colored a fox.

   ___Mike and Kim colored___
   ___two foxes.___

---

144 All in the Family

Directions: This is Andy's **family tree**. It shows all the people in his family. Use the words in the box to finish writing the names in Andy's family tree.

grandmother	mother
grandfather	father
aunt	uncle
brother	sister

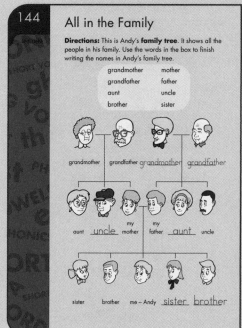

grandmother   grandfather   grandmother   grandfather

aunt   ___uncle___   my mother   my father   ___aunt___   uncle

sister   brother   me – Andy   ___sister___   ___brother___

Once Upon a Family 145

Directions: Write the family words in the blanks to complete the story.

One day, my family had a picnic. My

___grandmother___ baked chicken.

___grandfather___ baked some rolls.

My ___uncle___ Jack brought corn. My

___aunt___ made something green and white in a big dish. I ate the chicken my

___grandmother___ brought. I had two rolls made

by my ___grandfather___. My ___uncle___

gave me some corn. I liked it all! Then, my

___brother___ and I looked in the dish my

___aunt___ had brought. "Did you try it?"
I asked him.

"You're my big ___sister___," he said.
"You try it!" I put a tiny bit in my mouth. It tasted good!
But the dish was almost empty.

"It's terrible!" I said. "I'll eat the rest of it so you

won't have to. That's what a big ___sister___

is for!" My ___brother___ watched me eat it all.
I tried not to look too happy!

---

146 Where in the World?

Directions: Draw a line from each sentence to its picture. Then, complete each sentence with the word under the picture.

Example:
He is walking ___behind___ the tree.

outside

1. We stay ___inside___ when it rains.

behind

2. She drew a dog ___beside___ his house.

between

3. She stands ___between___ her friends.

across

4. They walked ___across___ the bridge.

around

5. Let the cat go ___outside___

beside

6. Draw a circle ___around___ the fish.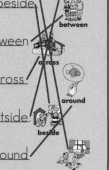

inside

Find That Cat! 147

Directions: Use a location word to tell where the cat is in each sentence.

Example:

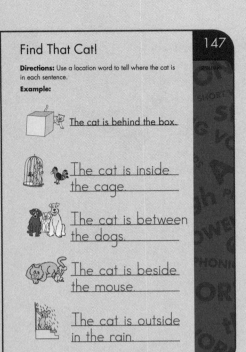

The cat is behind the box.

The cat is inside the cage.

The cat is between the dogs.

The cat is beside the mouse.

The cat is outside in the rain.

148 Heads or Tails?

Directions: Opposites are words which are different in every way. Use the opposite word from the box to complete these sentences.

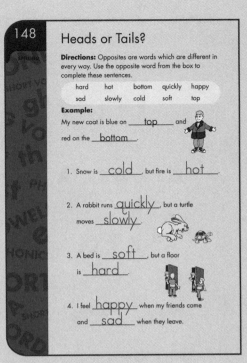

| hard | hot | bottom | quickly | happy |
| sad | slowly | cold | soft | top |

Example:

My new coat is blue on ___top___ and red on the ___bottom___.

1. Snow is ___cold___, but fire is ___hot___.

2. A rabbit runs ___quickly___, but a turtle moves ___slowly___.

3. A bed is ___soft___, but a floor is ___hard___.

4. I feel ___happy___ when my friends come and ___sad___ when they leave.

A Sweet Surprise 149

Directions: Write opposite words in the blanks to complete the story.

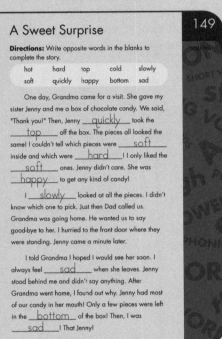

| hot | hard | top | cold | slowly |
| soft | quickly | happy | bottom | sad |

One day, Grandma came for a visit. She gave my sister Jenny and me a box of chocolate candy. We said, "Thank you!" Then, Jenny ___quickly___ took the ___top___ off the box. The pieces all looked the same! I couldn't tell which pieces were ___soft___ inside and which were ___hard___. I I only liked the ___soft___ ones. Jenny didn't care. She was ___happy___ to get any kind of candy!

I ___slowly___ looked at all the pieces. I didn't know which one to pick. Just then Dad called us. Grandma was going home. He wanted us to say good-bye to her. I hurried to the front door where they were standing. Jenny came a minute later.

I told Grandma I hoped I would see her soon. I always feel ___sad___ when she leaves. Jenny stood behind me and didn't say anything. After Grandma went home, I found out why. Jenny had most of our candy in her mouth! Only a few pieces were left in the ___bottom___ of the box! Then, I was ___sad___! That Jenny!

150 Tick, Tock, Time

The time between breakfast and lunch is **morning**.
The time between lunch and dinner is **afternoon**.
The time between dinner and bedtime is **evening**.

Directions: Write a time word from the box to complete each sentence. Use each word only once.

| evening | morning | today | tomorrow | afternoon |

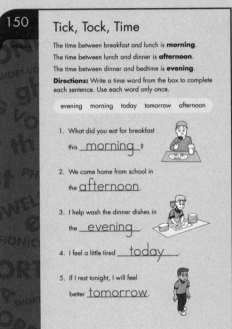

1. What did you eat for breakfast this ___morning___?

2. We came home from school in the ___afternoon___.

3. I help wash the dinner dishes in the ___evening___.

4. I feel a little tired ___today___.

5. If I rest tonight, I will feel better ___tomorrow___.

What Time Is It? 151

Directions: Write a sentence for these time words. Tell something you do at that time.

Example:

day

Every day I walk to school.

Answers will vary, but may include:

morning

I wake up early in the morning.

afternoon

I play outside in the afternoon.

evening

In the evening I watch T.V.

152 Review

Directions: Write the story below again and correct all the mistakes. Watch for words that are not spelled correctly, missing periods and question marks, question marks at the end of telling sentences and sentences with the wrong joining words.

One mourning, my granmother said I could have a pet mouse. That evening, we got my mouse at the pet store, or the next afernoon my mouse had babies! Now, I had nyne mouses! I really liked to wach them? I wanted to pick the babies up, and they were too little. When they get bigger, I have to give too mouses to my sisster.

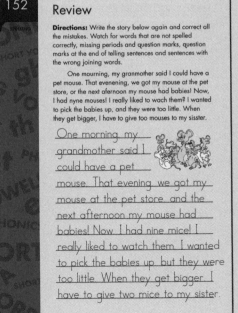

One morning, my grandmother said I could have a pet mouse. That evening, we got my mouse at the pet store, and the next afternoon my mouse had babies! Now I had nine mice! I really liked to watch them. I wanted to pick the babies up, but they were too little. When they get bigger, I have to give two mice to my sister.

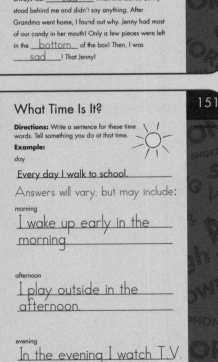

248

ANSWER KEY

---

154 — Shape Escape!

Directions: Complete each row by drawing the correct shape.

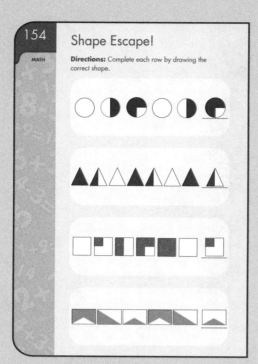

---

155 — Pick a Pattern

Mia likes to count by twos, threes, fours, fives, tens and hundreds.

Directions: Complete the number patterns.

1. 5, <u>10</u>, <u>15</u>, 20, <u>25</u>, <u>30</u>, 35, <u>40</u>, <u>45</u>, 50
2. 100, <u>200</u>, <u>300</u>, 400, <u>500</u>, <u>600</u>, <u>700</u>, 800, <u>900</u>
3. <u>2</u>, 4, 6, <u>8</u>, <u>10</u>, 12, <u>14</u>, 16, <u>18</u>, <u>20</u>
4. 10, <u>20</u>, <u>30</u>, 40, <u>50</u>, <u>60</u>, 70, <u>80</u>, 90
5. 4, <u>8</u>, 12, <u>16</u>, <u>20</u>, 24, <u>28</u>, 32, <u>36</u>, 40

Directions: Make up two of your own number patterns.
Answers will vary.
___, ___, ___, ___, ___

___, ___, ___, ___, ___

---

156 — All Aboard!

Ordinal numbers indicate order in a series, such as **first, second** or **third**.

Directions: Follow the instructions to color the train cars. The first car is the engine.

Color the third car **blue**.
Color the eighth car **green**.
Color the fifth car **orange**.
Color the sixth car **yellow**.
Color the fourth car **brown**.
Color the second car **purple**.
Color the first car **red**.
Color the seventh car **pink**.

---

157 — Add Attack!

Addition is "putting together" or adding two or more numbers to find the sum.

Directions: Add.

Example:

$$\begin{array}{r}2\\+5\\\hline7\end{array}$$

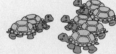

3 +4 7	6 +2 8	7 +1 8	8 +2 10	5 +4 9
8 +2 10	9 +5 14	10 +3 13	6 +6 12	4 +9 13
9 +3 12	8 +7 15	6 +5 11	7 +9 16	7 +6 13

---

158 — Add Attack: Forward and Back

The commutative property of addition states that even if the order of the numbers is changed in an addition sentence, the sum will stay tye same.

Example: 2 + 3 = 5
3 + 2 = 5

Directions: Look at the addition sentences below. Complete the addition sentences by writing the missing numerals.

5 + 4 = 9   3 + 1 = 4
4 + <u>5</u> = 9   1 + <u>3</u> = 4
2 + 6 = 8   6 + 1 = 7
6 + <u>2</u> = 8   1 + <u>6</u> = 7

Now try these:

6 + 3 = 9   10 + 2 = 12
<u>3</u> + <u>6</u> = 9   <u>2</u> + <u>10</u> = 12

Look at these sums. Can you think of two number sentences that would show the commutative property of addition.   Answers will vary.

___ + ___ = 7   ___ + ___ = 11
___ + ___ = 7   ___ + ___ = 11

---

159 — Add Attack: 3 or More Numbers

Directions: Add all the numbers to find the sum. Draw pictures to help or break up the problem into two smaller problems.

Example:

$$\begin{array}{r}1\\2\\+3\\\hline6\end{array}\qquad \begin{array}{r}2\\+5\end{array}\!\!\!>7 \quad \begin{array}{r}2\\+4\end{array}\!\!\!>\begin{array}{r}+6\\\hline13\end{array}$$

3 6 }9 +2 11	8 5 }9 +4 }9 17	3 1 }4 +5 }9 9	8 2 }10 +9 }9 19
2 8 }10 4 +3 }7 17	3 6 }9 5 +2 }7 16	4 1 }5 2 +5 }7 12	6 7 }13 3 +1 }4 17

160 — Take It Away!

Subtraction is "taking away" or subtracting one number from another to find the difference.

Directions: Subtract.

Example:

$$\begin{array}{r} 4 \\ -3 \\ \hline 1 \end{array}$$

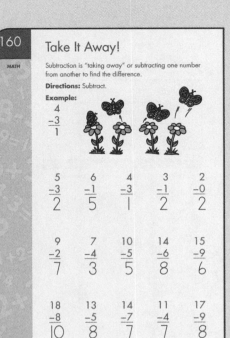

$$\begin{array}{r} 5 \\ -3 \\ \hline 2 \end{array} \quad \begin{array}{r} 6 \\ -1 \\ \hline 5 \end{array} \quad \begin{array}{r} 4 \\ -3 \\ \hline 1 \end{array} \quad \begin{array}{r} 3 \\ -1 \\ \hline 2 \end{array} \quad \begin{array}{r} 2 \\ -0 \\ \hline 2 \end{array}$$

$$\begin{array}{r} 9 \\ -2 \\ \hline 7 \end{array} \quad \begin{array}{r} 7 \\ -4 \\ \hline 3 \end{array} \quad \begin{array}{r} 10 \\ -5 \\ \hline 5 \end{array} \quad \begin{array}{r} 14 \\ -6 \\ \hline 8 \end{array} \quad \begin{array}{r} 15 \\ -9 \\ \hline 6 \end{array}$$

$$\begin{array}{r} 18 \\ -8 \\ \hline 10 \end{array} \quad \begin{array}{r} 13 \\ -5 \\ \hline 8 \end{array} \quad \begin{array}{r} 14 \\ -7 \\ \hline 7 \end{array} \quad \begin{array}{r} 11 \\ -4 \\ \hline 7 \end{array} \quad \begin{array}{r} 17 \\ -9 \\ \hline 8 \end{array}$$

161 — Find Your Place

The place value of a digit or numeral is shown by where it is in the number. For example, in the number **23**, 2 has the place value of **tens**, and 3 is **ones**.

Directions: Add the tens and ones and write your answers in the blanks.

Example:

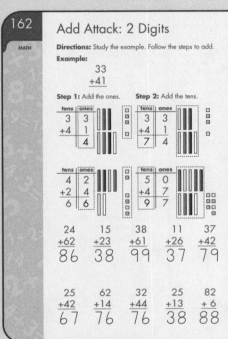

3 tens + 3 ones = 33

tens ones

7 tens + 5 ones = 75   4 tens + 0 ones = 40

2 tens + 3 ones = 23   8 tens + 1 one = 81

5 tens + 2 ones = 52   1 ten + 1 one = 11

5 tens + 4 ones = 54   6 tens + 3 ones = 63

Directions: Draw a line to the correct number.

6 tens + 7 ones → 67
4 tens + 2 ones → 42
8 tens + 0 ones → 80
7 tens + 3 ones → 73
5 tens + 1 one → 51

162 — Add Attack: 2 Digits

Directions: Study the example. Follow the steps to add.

Example:

$$\begin{array}{r} 33 \\ +41 \\ \hline \end{array}$$

Step 1: Add the ones.   **Step 2:** Add the tens.

tens	ones
3	3
+4	1
	4

tens	ones
3	3
+4	1
7	4

tens	ones
4	2
+2	4
6	6

tens	ones
5	0
+4	7
9	7

$$\begin{array}{r} 24 \\ +62 \\ \hline 86 \end{array} \quad \begin{array}{r} 15 \\ +23 \\ \hline 38 \end{array} \quad \begin{array}{r} 38 \\ +61 \\ \hline 99 \end{array} \quad \begin{array}{r} 11 \\ +26 \\ \hline 37 \end{array} \quad \begin{array}{r} 37 \\ +42 \\ \hline 79 \end{array}$$

$$\begin{array}{r} 25 \\ +42 \\ \hline 67 \end{array} \quad \begin{array}{r} 62 \\ +14 \\ \hline 76 \end{array} \quad \begin{array}{r} 32 \\ +44 \\ \hline 76 \end{array} \quad \begin{array}{r} 25 \\ +13 \\ \hline 38 \end{array} \quad \begin{array}{r} 82 \\ +6 \\ \hline 88 \end{array}$$

163 — Add Attack: 2 Digits

Directions: Add the total points scored in each game. Remember to add **ones** first and **tens** second.

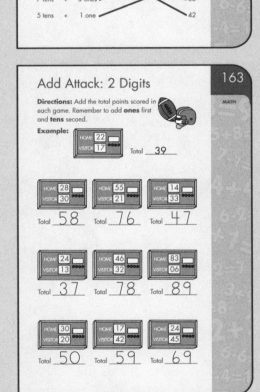

Example:

HOME 22 VISITOR 17   Total 39

HOME 28 / VISITOR 30   Total 58
HOME 55 / VISITOR 21   Total 76
HOME 14 / VISITOR 33   Total 47

HOME 24 / VISITOR 13   Total 37
HOME 46 / VISITOR 32   Total 78
HOME 83 / VISITOR 06   Total 89

HOME 30 / VISITOR 20   Total 50
HOME 17 / VISITOR 42   Total 59
HOME 24 / VISITOR 45   Total 69

164 — Add Attack: 2 Digits

Addition is "putting together" or adding two or more numbers to find the sum. Regrouping is using **ten ones** to form **one ten**, **ten tens** to form **one 100**, **fifteen ones** to form **one ten** and **five ones** and so on.

Directions: Study the examples. Follow the steps to add.

Example:

$$\begin{array}{r} 14 \\ +8 \\ \hline \end{array}$$

Step 1: Add the ones.   **Step 2:** Regroup the tens.   **Step 3:** Add the tens.

tens	ones
1	4
+	8
	12

tens	ones
1	
1	4
+	8
	2

tens	ones
1	
1	4
+	8
2	2

tens	ones
1	
1	6
+3	7
5	3

tens	ones
1	
3	8
+5	3
9	1

tens	ones
1	
2	4
+4	7
7	1

$$\begin{array}{r} 28 \\ +17 \\ \hline 45 \end{array} \quad \begin{array}{r} 32 \\ +38 \\ \hline 70 \end{array} \quad \begin{array}{r} 54 \\ +25 \\ \hline 79 \end{array} \quad \begin{array}{r} 19 \\ +55 \\ \hline 74 \end{array} \quad \begin{array}{r} 44 \\ +48 \\ \hline 92 \end{array}$$

165 — Add Attack: 2 Digits

Directions: Add the total points scored in the game. Remember to add the ones, regroup, and then add the tens.

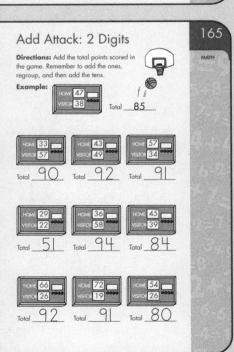

Example:

HOME 47 / VISITOR 38   Total 85

HOME 33 / VISITOR 57   Total 90
HOME 43 / VISITOR 49   Total 92
HOME 57 / VISITOR 34   Total 91

HOME 29 / VISITOR 22   Total 51
HOME 36 / VISITOR 58   Total 94
HOME 45 / VISITOR 39   Total 84

HOME 66 / VISITOR 26   Total 92
HOME 72 / VISITOR 19   Total 91
HOME 54 / VISITOR 26   Total 80

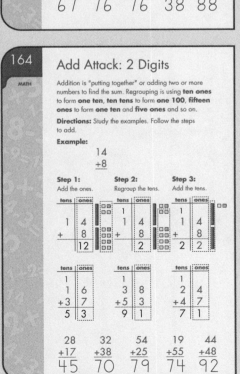

166 Take It Away: 2 Digits

Directions: Study the example. Follow the steps to subtract.

Example:

```
  28
 -14
```

Step 1: Subtract the ones. **Step 2:** Subtract the tens.

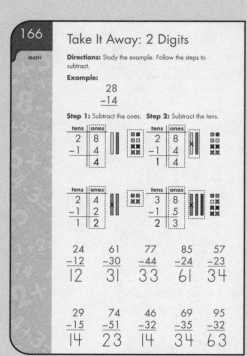

tens	ones
2	8
-1	4
1	4

```
 24    61    77    85    57
-12   -30   -44   -24   -23
 12    31    33    61    34

 29    74    46    69    95
-15   -51   -32   -35   -32
 14    23    14    34    63
```

167 Take It Away: 2 Digits

Directions: Study the steps for subtracting. Solve the problems using the steps.

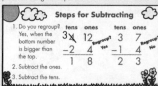

Steps for Subtracting
1. Do you regroup? Yes, when the bottom number is bigger than the top.
2. Subtract the ones.
3. Subtract the tens.

```
tens ones    tens ones    tens ones
 4    7       6    4       5    3
-2    8      -3    4      -3    9
 1    9       3    0       1    4

 56    83    43    75    91
-27   -47   -39   -53   -18
 29    36     4    22    73

 73    35    67    26    68
-66   -14   -58   - 7   -45
  7    21     9    19    23
```

168 Review

Directions: Add or subtract. Use regrouping when needed. Always do ones first and tens last.

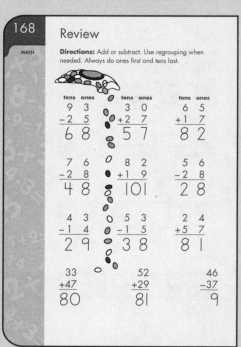

```
tens ones    tens ones    tens ones
 9    3       3    0       6    5
-2    5      +2    7      +1    7
 6    8       5    7       8    2

 7    6       8    2       5    6
-2    8      +1    9      -2    8
 4    8      10    1       2    8

 4    3       5    3       2    4
-1    4      -1    5      +5    7
 2    9       3    8       8    1

 33           52           46
+47          +29          -37
 80           81            9
```

169 Hundreds of Places

The place value of a digit or numeral is shown by where it is in the number. For example, in the number **123**, **1** has the place value of **hundreds**, **2** is **tens** and **3** is **ones**.

Directions: Study the examples. Then, write the missing numbers in the blanks.

Examples:

2 hundreds + 3 tens + 6 ones =

hundreds	tens	ones	
2	3	6	= 236

1 hundreds + 4 tens + 9 ones =

hundreds	tens	ones	
1	4	9	= 149

	hundreds	tens	ones	total
3 hundreds + 4 tens + 8 ones =	3	4	8	348
2 hundreds + 1 tens + 7 ones =	2	1	7	217
6 hundreds + 3 tens + 5 ones =	6	3	5	635
4 hundreds + 7 tens + 9 ones =	4	7	9	479
2 hundreds + 9 tens + 4 ones =	2	9	4	294
4 hundreds + 5 tens + 6 ones =	4	5	6	456
3 hundreds + 1 ten + 3 ones =	3	1	3	313
3 hundreds + 5 ten + 7 ones =	3	5	7	357
6 hundreds + 2 ten + 8 ones =	6	2	8	628

170 Add Attack: 3 Digits

Directions: Study the examples. Follow the steps to add.

Example:

Step 1: Add the ones. **Step 2:** Add the tens. **Step 3:** Add the hundreds.

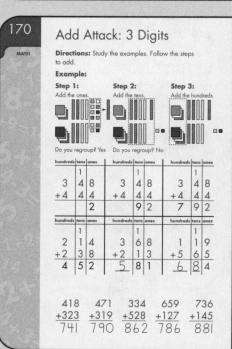

Do you regroup? Yes   Do you regroup? No

hundreds	tens	ones
	1	
3	4	8
+4	4	4
		2

hundreds	tens	ones
	1	
3	4	8
+4	4	4
	9	2

hundreds	tens	ones
	1	
3	4	8
+4	4	4
7	9	2

```
hundreds tens ones
 2    1    4
+2    3    8
 4    5    2

 3    6    8
+2    1    3
 5    8    1

 1    1    9
+5    6    5
 6    8    4

 418    471    334    659    736
+323   +319   +528   +127   +145
 741    790    862    786    881
```

171 Add Attack: 3 Digits

Directions: Study the example. Follow the steps to add. Regroup when needed.

Step 1: Add the ones.
Step 2: Add the tens.
Step 3: Add the hundreds.

10 = 1 ten + 0 ones

hundreds	tens	ones
	1	1
3	4	8
+4	5	4
8	0	2

```
 348    172    575    623    369
+214   +418   +329   +268   +533
 562    590    904    891    902

 411    423    639    624    272
+299   +169   +177   +368   +469
 710    592    816    992    741
```

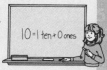

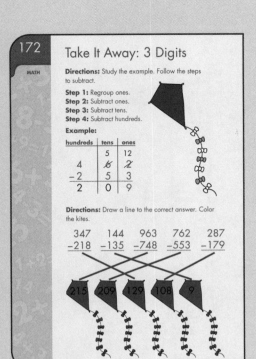

172 Take It Away: 3 Digits

MATH

Directions: Study the example. Follow the steps to subtract.

Step 1: Regroup ones.
Step 2: Subtract ones.
Step 3: Subtract tens.
Step 4: Subtract hundreds.

Example:

hundreds	tens	ones
	5	12
4	6̶	2̶
−2	5	3
2	0	9

Directions: Draw a line to the correct answer. Color the kites.

347	144	963	762	287
−218	−135	−748	−553	−179

215   209   129   108   9

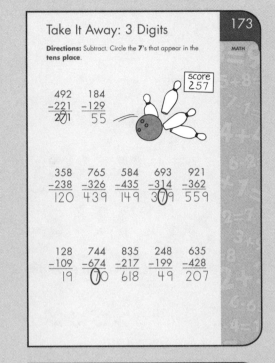

173 Take It Away: 3 Digits

MATH

Directions: Subtract. Circle the **7**'s that appear in the **tens place**.

score 257

492	184
−221	−129
2⑦1	55

358	765	584	693	921
−238	−326	−435	−314	−362
120	439	149	3⑦9	559

128	744	835	248	635
−109	−674	−217	−199	−428
19	⑦0	618	49	207

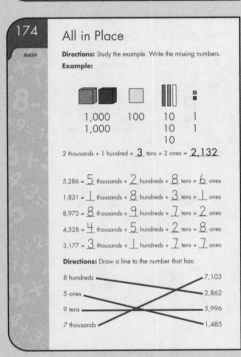

174 All in Place

MATH

Directions: Study the example. Write the missing numbers.

Example:

1,000   100   10   1
1,000   10   1
                10

2 thousands + 1 hundred + **3** tens + 2 ones = **2,132**

5,286 = **5** thousands + **2** hundreds + **8** tens + **6** ones
1,831 = **1** thousands + **8** hundreds + **3** tens + **1** ones
8,972 = **8** thousands + **9** hundreds + **7** tens + **2** ones
4,528 = **4** thousands + **5** hundreds + **2** tens + **8** ones
3,177 = **3** thousands + **1** hundreds + **7** tens + **7** ones

Directions: Draw a line to the number that has:

8 hundreds ——— 7,103
5 ones ——— 2,862
9 tens ——— 5,996
7 thousands ——— 1,485

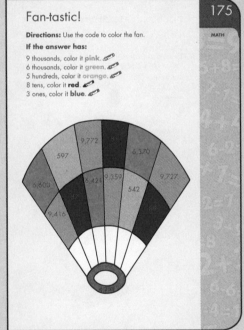

175 Fan-tastic!

MATH

Directions: Use the code to color the fan.

If the answer has:
9 thousands, color it **pink**.
6 thousands, color it **green**.
5 hundreds, color it **orange**.
8 tens, color it **red**.
3 ones, color it **blue**.

9,772   6,370
597
6,600   6,421   9,359   9,727
542
9,416

176 Take a Bite

MATH

A graph is a drawing that shows information about numbers.

Directions: Count the apples in each row. Color the boxes to show how many apples have bites taken out of them.

Example:

1 2 3 4 5 6 7 8

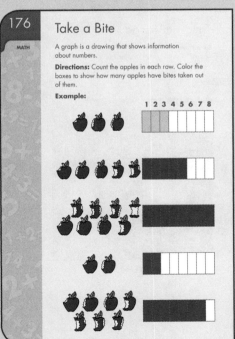

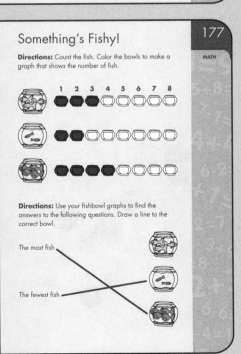

177 Something's Fishy!

MATH

Directions: Count the fish. Color the bowls to make a graph that shows the number of fish.

1 2 3 4 5 6 7 8

Directions: Use your fishbowl graphs to find the answers to the following questions. Draw a line to the correct bowl.

The most fish

The fewest fish

178 Bunches of Bugs

Multiplication is a short way to find the sum of adding the same number a certain amount of times. For example, **4 x 7 = 28** instead of **7 + 7 + 7 + 7 = 28**.

Directions: Study the example. Solve the problems.

Example:

3 + 3 + 3 = 9
3 threes = 9
3 x 3 = 9

7 + 7 = 14
2 sevens = 14
2 x 7 = 14

4 + 4 + 4 + 4 = 16
4 fours = 16
4 x 4 = 16

5 + 5 = 10
2 fives = 10
2 x 5 = 10

2 + 2 + 2 + 2 = 8
4 twos = 8
4 x 2 = 8

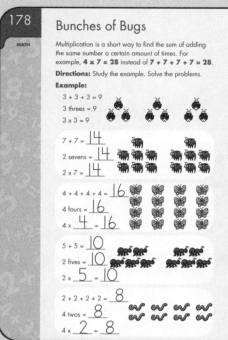

179 Good Times!

Directions: Study the example. Draw the groups and write the total.

Example:

3 x 2
2 + 2 + 2 = 6

3 x 4
4 + 4 + 4 = 12

2 x 5
5 + 5 = 10

5 x 3
3 + 3 + 3 + 3 + 3 = 15

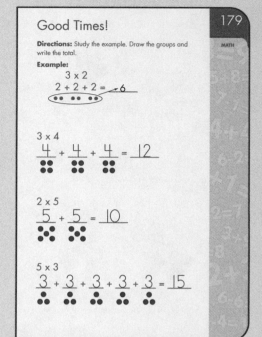

180 Focus on Fractions

A fraction is a number that names part of a whole, such as ½ or ⅓.

Directions: Study the examples. Color the correct fraction of each shape.

Examples:

shaded part 1
equal parts 2
½ (one-half) shaded

shaded part 1
equal parts 3
⅓ (one-third) shaded

shaded part 1
equal parts 4
¼ (one-fourth) shaded

Color:
⅓ **red**

Color:
¼ **blue**

Color:
½ **orange**

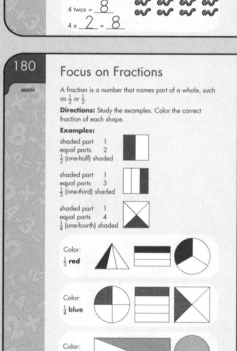

181 Made in the Shade

Directions: Study the examples. Circle the fraction that shows the shaded part. Then, circle the fraction that shows the white part.

Examples:

shaded $\frac{1}{4}$ $\frac{1}{3}$ (½) white $\frac{1}{3}$ (½) $\frac{1}{4}$ shaded $\frac{1}{4}$ $\frac{1}{2}$ (¾) white (¼) $\frac{2}{3}$ $\frac{1}{2}$

shaded $\frac{1}{4}$ (⅓) $\frac{1}{2}$ white $\frac{2}{4}$ (⅔) $\frac{2}{2}$ shaded (¾) $\frac{1}{3}$ $\frac{3}{2}$ white $\frac{1}{2}$ (¼) $\frac{1}{3}$

shaded $\frac{2}{3}$ (²⁄₄) $\frac{2}{2}$ white $\frac{1}{3}$ (²⁄₄) $\frac{2}{2}$ shaded $\frac{2}{4}$ (⅔) $\frac{2}{2}$ white $\frac{1}{2}$ $\frac{1}{4}$ (⅓)

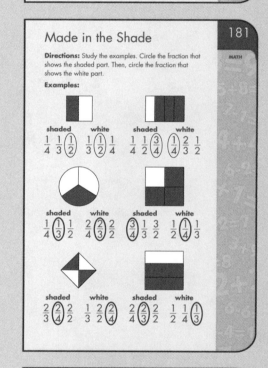

182 Get in Shape!

Geometry is mathematics that has to do with lines and shapes.

Directions: Color the shapes.

Color the triangles **blue**.
Color the circles **red**.
Color the squares green.
Color the rectangles pink.

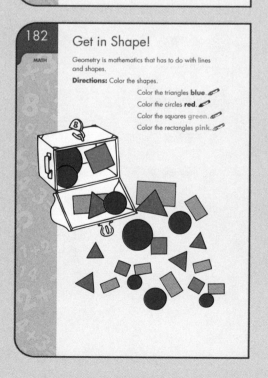

183 Tangram Tango

Directions: Cut out the tangram below. Mix up the pieces. Try to put it back together into a square.

253

185 — Measuring Up

MATH

Directions: Cut out the ruler. Measure each object to the nearest inch.

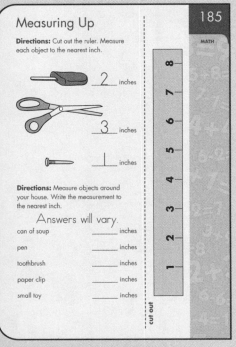

- screwdriver: **2** inches
- scissors: **3** inches
- nail: **1** inches

Directions: Measure objects around your house. Write the measurement to the nearest inch.

Answers will vary.

- can of soup _____ inches
- pen _____ inches
- toothbrush _____ inches
- paper clip _____ inches
- small toy _____ inches

187 — Catch of the Day

MATH

Directions: Use the ruler to measure the fish to the nearest inch.

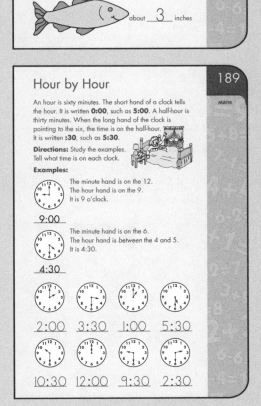

- about **4** inches
- about **1** inches
- about **2** inches
- about **1** inches
- about **3** inches
- about **3** inches

188 — Centimeter Sense

MATH

A centimeter is a unit of length in the metric system. There are 2.54 centimeters in an inch.

Directions: Use a centimeter ruler to measure the crayons to the nearest centimeter.

Example: The first crayon is about 7 centimeters long.

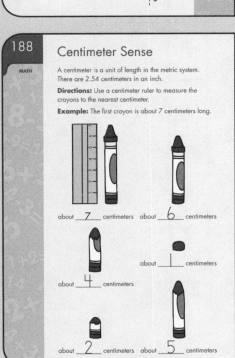

- about **7** centimeters
- about **6** centimeters
- about **4** centimeters
- about **1** centimeters
- about **2** centimeters
- about **5** centimeters

189 — Hour by Hour

MATH

An hour is sixty minutes. The short hand of a clock tells the hour. It is written **0:00**, such as **5:00**. A half-hour is thirty minutes. When the long hand of the clock is pointing to the six, the time is on the half-hour. It is written **:30**, such as **5:30**.

Directions: Study the examples. Tell what time is on each clock.

Examples:

The minute hand is on the 12.
The hour hand is on the 9.
It is 9 o'clock.

9:00

The minute hand is on the 6.
The hour hand is *between* the 4 and 5.
It is 4:30.

4:30

- 2:00
- 3:30
- 1:00
- 5:30
- 10:30
- 12:00
- 9:30
- 2:30

190 — Time's Up!

MATH

The minute hand of a clock takes 5 minutes to move from one number to the next. Start at the 12 and count by fives to tell how many minutes it is past the hour.

Directions: Study the examples. Tell what time is on each clock.

Examples: 9:10   8:25

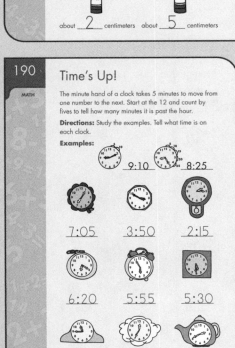

- 7:05
- 3:50
- 2:15
- 6:20
- 5:55
- 5:30
- 11:45
- 12:35
- 2:40

191 — Telling Time

MATH

Time can also be shown as fractions. 30 minutes = $\frac{1}{2}$ hour.

Directions: Shade the fraction of each clock and tell how many minutes you have shaded.

Example:

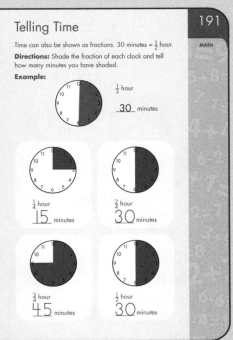

- $\frac{1}{2}$ hour — **30** minutes
- $\frac{1}{4}$ hour — **15** minutes
- $\frac{2}{4}$ hour — **30** minutes
- $\frac{3}{4}$ hour — **45** minutes
- $\frac{1}{2}$ hour — **30** minutes

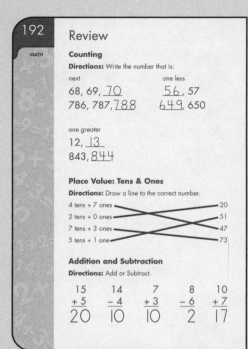

192 MATH

Review

Counting

Directions: Write the number that is:

next
68, 69, _70_

one less
_56_, 57

786, 787, _788_

_649_, 650

one greater
12, _13_

843, _844_

Place Value: Tens & Ones

Directions: Draw a line to the correct number.

4 tens + 7 ones — 20
2 tens + 0 ones — 51
7 tens + 3 ones — 47
5 tens + 1 one — 73

Addition and Subtraction

Directions: Add or Subtract.

15	14	7	8	10
+5	−4	+3	−6	+7
20	10	10	2	17

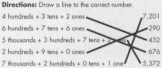

193 MATH

Review

2-Digit Addition and Subtraction

Directions: Add or subtract using regrouping, if needed.

66	38	87	52	40
−37	+18	−69	−15	+17
29	56	18	37	57

84	65	99	61	56
+17	+14	−48	−36	+46
101	79	51	25	102

Place Value: Hundreds and Thousands

Directions: Draw a line to the correct number.

4 hundreds + 3 tens + 2 ones — 7,201
6 hundreds + 7 tens + 6 ones — 290
5 thousands + 3 hundreds + 7 tens + 2 ones — 432
2 hundreds + 9 tens + 0 ones — 676
7 thousands + 2 hundreds + 0 tens + 1 one — 5,372

3-Digit Addition and Subtraction

Directions: Add or subtract, remembering to regroup, if needed.

458	793	822	528	697
−248	−414	−460	+319	+108
210	379	362	847	805

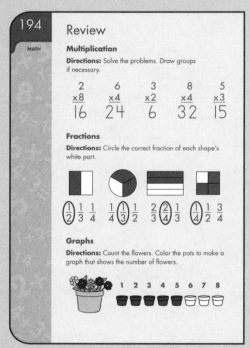

194 MATH

Review

Multiplication

Directions: Solve the problems. Draw groups if necessary.

2	6	3	8	5
×8	×4	×2	×4	×3
16	24	6	32	15

Fractions

Directions: Circle the correct fraction of each shape's white part.

(1/2) 1/3 1/4   1/4 (1/3) 1/2   2/3 (2/1) 1/4   (1/4) 1/2 3/4

Graphs

Directions: Count the flowers. Color the pots to make a graph that shows the number of flowers.

1 2 3 4 5 6 7 8

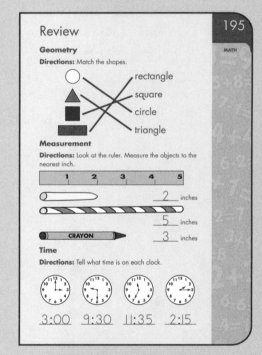

195 MATH

Review

Geometry

Directions: Match the shapes.

rectangle
square
circle
triangle

Measurement

Directions: Look at the ruler. Measure the objects to the nearest inch.

1 2 3 4 5

_2_ inches

_5_ inches

CRAYON
_3_ inches

Time

Directions: Tell what time is on each clock.

_3:00_   _9:30_   _11:35_   _2:15_

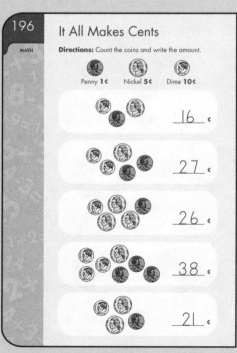

196 MATH

It All Makes Cents

Directions: Count the coins and write the amount.

Penny 1¢   Nickel 5¢   Dime 10¢

_16_ ¢

_27_ ¢

_26_ ¢

_38_ ¢

_21_ ¢

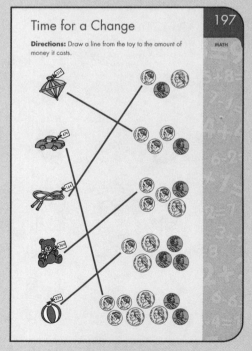

197 MATH

Time for a Change

Directions: Draw a line from the toy to the amount of money it costs.

198 | Counting Coins

MATH

A quarter is worth **25¢**.

Directions: Count the coins and write the amounts.

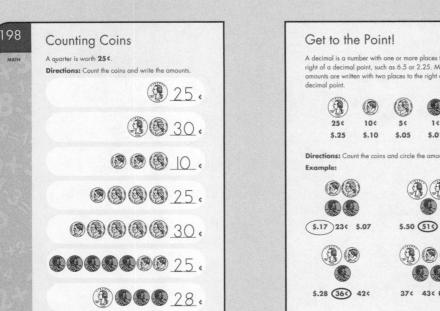

25 ¢

30 ¢

10 ¢

25 ¢

30 ¢

25 ¢

28 ¢

36 ¢

199 | Get to the Point!

MATH

A decimal is a number with one or more places to the right of a decimal point, such as 6.5 or 2.25. Money amounts are written with two places to the right of the decimal point.

25¢	10¢	5¢	1¢
$.25	$.10	$.05	$.01

Directions: Count the coins and circle the amount shown.

Example:

(**$.17**) 23¢ $.07 $.50 (**51¢**) 61¢

$.28 (**36¢**) 42¢   37¢ 43¢ (**$.47**)

200 | Dollar Days

MATH

One dollar equals 100 cents. It is written $1.00.

Directions: Count the money and write the amounts.

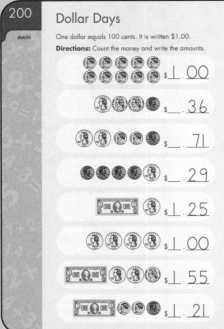

$ 1.00

$ .36

$ .71

$ .29

$ 1.25

$ 1.00

$ 1.55

$ 1.21

201 | Add It Up

MATH

Directions: Write the amount of money using decimals. Then, add to find the total amount.

Example:

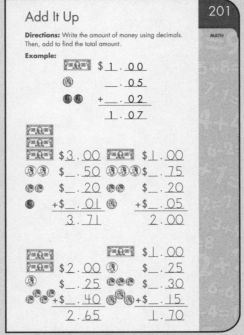

$ 1.00
.05
+ .02
1.07

$3.00 $1.00
$ .50 $ .75
$ .20 $ .20
+$ .01   +$ .05
3.71   2.00

$2.00 $1.00
$ .25 $ .25
+$ .40 $ .30
2.65   +$ .15
               1.70

202 | A Day at the Park

MATH

Directions: Tell if you add, subtract or multiply. Then, write the answer.

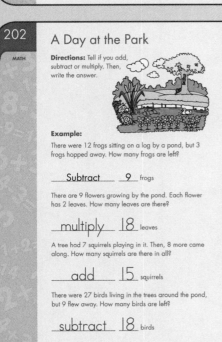

Example:

There were 12 frogs sitting on a log by a pond, but 3 frogs hopped away. How many frogs are left?

__Subtract__ _9_ frogs

There are 9 flowers growing by the pond. Each flower has 2 leaves. How many leaves are there?

__multiply__ _18_ leaves

A tree had 7 squirrels playing in it. Then, 8 more came along. How many squirrels are there in all?

__add__ _15_ squirrels

There were 27 birds living in the trees around the pond, but 9 flew away. How many birds are left?

__subtract__ _18_ birds

203 | Time to Solve It

MATH

Directions: Solve each problem.

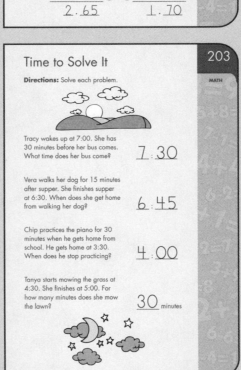

Tracy wakes up at 7:00. She has 30 minutes before her bus comes. What time does her bus come?

_7_ : _30_

Vera walks her dog for 15 minutes after supper. She finishes supper at 6:30. When does she get home from walking her dog?

_6_ : _45_

Chip practices the piano for 30 minutes when he gets home from school. He gets home at 3:30. When does he stop practicing?

_4_ : _00_

Tanya starts mowing the grass at 4:30. She finishes at 5:00. For how many minutes does she mow the lawn?

_30_ minutes

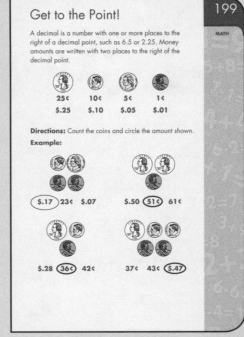

256

ANSWER KEY

204 Toy Time

MATH

Directions: Read each problem. Use the pictures to help you solve the problems.

Ben bought a ball. He had 11¢ left. How much money did he have at the start? **40** ¢

Tara has 75¢. She buys a car. How much money does she have left? **30** ¢

Leah wants to buy a doll and a ball. She has 80¢. How much more money does she need? **8** ¢

Jacob has 95¢. He buys the car and the ball. How much more money does he need to buy a doll for his sister? **38** ¢

Kim paid three quarters, one dime and three pennies for a hat. How much did it cost? **88** ¢